MUSCULAR POETRY

MUSCULAR POETRY II

BY KEMO CHEN

MUSCULAR POETRY II

iUniverse books may be ordered through booksellers or by contacting:

iUniverse
1663 Liberty Drive
Bloomington, IN 47403
www.iuniverse.com
1-800-Authors (1-800-288-4677)

ISBN: 978-1-5320-9557-3 (sc)
ISBN: 978-1-5320-9558-0 (e)

Print information available on the last page.

iUniverse rev. date: 02/19/2020

What The Hell Is This

Poetry.

A collection of poems for all of us.

Poems that express the truths of being a modern man, without

artifice, delusion or camouflage. It is not the poems of the wonder of nature,

flowers and trees, sublime love, unwarranted optimism.

It is instead about the inner journey to find the best of ourselves

sometimes at great cost and loss. The vagaries of the essential struggle

to achieve, love, overcome adversity, find peace of mind.

And, the ability to battle the forces, that come like waves to drown

our dreams. Find the wisdom to fight for outcomes that give our lives

meaning. It is poetry, declaring, you are not alone, unless you want to be,

and knowing that either way, the choice is the essence of your free will.

This MUSCULAR POETRY that is transparent with its message, simply proclaiming that a man can seek many things, all that have their

consequences,intended and not. But, there are other matters often

not on the list of achievements and concerns, and, that is happiness

and some measure of joy.

If there is bliss out there, it is as much a birthright and part of the genetic

code as fortitude, courage, and grit.

You will not like them all, to be sure.

But, perhaps, a few of them will touch you, humor you.

Some may reveal something you did not know.

And maybe, just maybe, some of this will guide you to someplace

you want to discover.

Here is to that inner journey, and your right to pursue it

KC

2020

How Toxic Are You

Do you suppress your emotion?

Mask your distress?

Always present a game face?

Be tough when confronted?

Actually fight?

Show violence in speech when agitated?

Be in control?

Hardly ever cry?

If any of those are you

You have become entwined in

Toxic masculinity

Declared from university classes and studies of what we have done

To make a woman's life more difficult by being men like that

The later day feminist is no longer about their

Equality and pay, or any range of issues that were

Compelling back in the day

Now men must be retrained, and even young boys taught

That these traits are not ingrained but taught by other men

To encase all men in a collective psyche that can only do harm

As we move into another age

It is toxic to be tough, gritty and hard
Toxic to talk back and fight for what you believe
Toxic to disagree and express it loud
Toxic to stand erect than be beaten to your knees

What is toxic to them is
Bravery and courage
Steadfastness and devotion
Gravitas and seriousness
Adaptation and resolve
Silence and contemplation
To all of us

And there may be some alternate universe
Where values are upended
No gender designations, everyone reacts the same to
Stimuli in the atmosphere, regardless of the X or Y's
Where everyone is open hearted, nice as can be, and
just

I suppose we will need a declaration of the rights of men
To be, exactly how we are, free to yell when angry, or hit a
guy in a bar, stand for our values and even go to war,
encourage sons to be like us, and practice what we preach
And be yielding, open and sensitive, when needed to as well

But the pundits, feminists, and believers in Toxic Masculinity
Can all go straight to Hell!

A Silent Poet Laureate

Outrageous to believe
A poet who is dubbed as laureate by
City by the sea
Will not read his works aloud
When asked by an interviewer

Two doctorates, he has
A double PHD
A waistline over 50 inches, no belt to notch it seems
Writes of cows and goats, and farm machines
bucolic rural scenes

Later works from on the farm
Steinbeck and Saroyan themes
Heart attacks make the later rounds
And the big "C" slays a few as well
Eventually,he is city bound and his
Contemplative Jimmy Stewart turns
Dark, as the horizon comes into view
Over the Hudson River, as the sun sets
At the end of 57th street

This poet they have chosen
Can write volumes to recite on his victory
Tour

A laureate who will not read
His poems to just a few, only to the throngs
Is his current point of view

There are no known poets, really, anymore
Even the good dead ones are forgotten
Bukowski, Maya, Rod McKuen, Langston Hughes
To cite a few
You would freeze in January at Target, until you would
Find five shoppers who could recall a single name, and
Die waiting for someone to recite anything but Mary and
her Lamb
So to have a man selected to be named
A poet of some fame to fail to read except at a reading
At a salon
When he is ready to expound
Says all we need to know, about hubris, insularity
And lunacy

CARE FREE

Can you ever be
truly,
Without worry, of next and when,
In that moment wherever you are
Care free

Chatting up a man who carves wood behind a roadside shack
in Morea, and sells boxes that hold cigars, paper clips, or colored pebbles
His mind in his wood and blades
while yours is away in some distant office space

A high tide brings 10 footers and
The sea fills with black suited men
intent on the wave to ride
all you see is that woman who rejected you
and your brain is awash with the firing of neurons that
bring both anger and regret
as you fall off the board
again and again

what genome do they all have
where whatever is a bother or a pain is dissipated by
a simple willfulness to be

for one moment, afternoon, or sunset

without a single care

letting them be free of the eternal prison

of remorse, regret, and

the tyranny of preparing for the next thing.

Containment

There are always boundaries
Closing in on us
Keeping us from harm or straying into another's
Space or place
Imposed, unfenced barriers

On my back on another cloudless January
Afternoon
Crunches, shirtless
A yellow jacket hovers on the periphery of my small space
Each crunch,it comes closer
Bringing Proustian memories of swollen cheeks and neck
From some single sting
Unbearable injections in my ass, ice packs

Truman and MacArthur contained the Chinese along the
38th
Johnson and Westmoreland the Vietcong at the 17th
Lines drawn, not to be crossed by Commies, not without
retaliation

There is danger along those lines
Existential threats
Stakes high enough to respond

The stuff of first strikes, beyond old Clausewitz, or
Metternich and
Even Kissinger tomes

That bee gets closer
I have no patience for it
One step neutralizes the threat

One hundred more crunches
In a place without buzzing or danger
And an odd calm rises

It Can Be Lonely on Xmas

Working Xmas is less miserable than watching
Television alone
There is some cheer, stale coffee, and bakery goods
A few smiles

No one groans, in this brotherhood of misfits, punching
some biometric clock
hugging, the man hugs, and humming old tunes to yourself
Then there is nothing left to do, and it gets too uncomfortable
to stay
And I am off with the pretense there is something awaiting me
If only the ruse of it.

A short nap before sunset
A run on the hard sand
A horizon washed orange
walkers in Santa hats, and scarfs
Mostly arm in arm

I wonder,if I am dreaming this
And I am still asleep and it is all memory
Is this day better or has it been worse

Calderon invented Segismundo in 1635
To wonder what is and is not

Is it all a dream anyway, locked in our minds
La Vida es un sueno?

Then a dog barks, there is always a dog
Yapping and crapping by the sea
Not what I would dream

Awake I am to the orange sky, the hard sand
That empty apartment and the utter silence
Of another Xmas night alone.

THE THREE REVOLUTIONS

I missed the great three revolutions
Where what was once changed for man forever
Abraham was the first, there was one God
Christ the second, John 3:16
All men are created equal, was the third, with the American
Revolution

Inside a slopped brow skull the brain grew
And man finds believing in something beyond him offers
Something
Prayers go to trees, the objects in the sky, animals,

Superstition reigns
Something to offer guidance and solace
Elevate some to monarchs, and the inequity of ruling
everyone else
Faith mostly blind backed by might and ruthless treatment
of everyone

Abraham has a family finally over 90
Spreads the word
Offers his son, after a three day walk to Mt. Moriah
Idols come and go
Dynasties stay with their Gods, Rome rules,
Abraham's God morphs into the covenant with Moses'

Few adopt one God, or the commandments
Jews rule, but mostly suffer, temples rise and are destroyed

And into this Christ arrives
A Jew, who is not only a believer, but the redeemer
More hardship, sacrifice, Roman atrocities,
And yet, Christianity becomes the new world view
Adopted by Church and State, wages wars, Crusades,
Supports divine rights, feudalism and more

Thought shifts, slowly and in only some places
We are all equal and designed to be free by that same God
that spoke to
Abraham and sent us Christ
All faiths have standing, there is some contract between
us all
No one is divinely chosen to rule, the only will is that of
the people
And their destiny is in their hands

For every Washington there is a Robespierre. Revolution
begets battles
blood, reaction, and often a return to the status quo ante
bellum or worse
Nascent democracy holds, barely
as authoritarianism sprouts out of it,
births totalitarianism that holds a grip on a third of the
world.

Our brains now developed, now out of the caves,
writing on phones and devices, no cave paintings
Giving our souls over to what next
Quantum machines, robots that tells us what to do or where
to go
As it rolls across the floor onto our beds

Who is God talking to
Is there some Abraham in our midst, unrevealed
Does the promised return of Messiah usher in the next and
final
Revolution
Or
Is there nothing ahead at all, no grand opening, no celestial
red carpet
Only this struggle to find something that makes us feel alive
And that may be enough, anyway

SUMMERTIME AT 42ND AND 6TH

The lions have seen it all
Fist fights between school boys throwing back packs
into the street
A couple of women pushing walkers up the library steps
That long legged gal in the black skirt, with the leg slit
Rubbing it against her boyfriends thigh, as she pulls his hair
So she can French kiss him

They might roar in disgust, these concrete centurions
As a black man, over 300 pounds, lies face down, asleep on
this warm night, with
his face seeping between the grates
where the subways subterranean fumes rise to fill his nostrils

or listen to the theme from the Coppola's family
the Godfather played on an alto sax
as the ragged impresario plays it well, and has a case of more
change
than you could conjure or ever earn
wondering why someone wouldn't throw the guy a buck,
instead of a quarter

and they might rip apart that vendor
who sells you a drink and a soft pretzel
you give him a ten and you get

two dollars in change

"Hey buddy, I gave you a ten!"
"Yea, So, Boss?"
The drink is two bucks and the pretzel is 8.

NY NY what a wonderful town.

What's the Frequency?

Kenneth !
Screamed the deranged William Tager to the
Anchorman, Dan Rather, in Manhattan in 1986
It was a transmitter in his head that he was talking to he said
some blamed Rather for being scrambled himself
Tager shot a stagehand at a later date

Insanity rubbing up against civility
Society shrugs and is frozen into inaction
Rather knows only the vibration of that moment
He moves on to Courage

All of us at 62 hertz, small vibes on a planet 7.83Hz
In a universe at 432Hz

This humming, discordant in most searching for
An inner resonance that is tuned in to something or
someone
These Solfeggio vibrations can lift us from 396 Hz to rid
of us fear
And guilt
To 528Hz to repair DNA onward
To a vibrational nirvana of 852 Hz
Perhaps there to find an anointed one who can
Launch a new spiritual order

Crap

What was Mother Teresa's frequency 70Hz, or

For that matter, FDR, Torquemada, or Stalin?

Does William know more as a schizoid than the rest of us

Are we so immune, out of tune, unlike R.E.M. who made a tune about it

What corner are we in losing more than our religion

or some street corner, somewhere, vibrating a universal frequency to each

other

Be kinder, dude

Raise your frequency a few HZ

Be quiet, when you can

Don't frighten yourself or others

Be on the way to a higher vibe

How insane is that,

Kenneth.

THANK YOU LILLIAN

For being there in Miami in February 1933
And wearing a hat, and being somewhat taller than most
And standing by Mr. Astor's yacht, waiting to see FDR.

He was off on a cruise to the Caribbean, a few weeks before
his Inaugural
You thought him robust and energetic, even in his chair
But what was next you could not know from behind you

Shots fired from a .32 revolver, worth 8 bucks, in the hands
of a poor Italian immigrant, who laid bricks to get by
and hated FDR, the rich and anyone doing better, or so it
seemed to
Giuseppe Zangara, in his distorted worldview

He had stretched his full five feet, and stood on a metal chair
to get over your hat
And see FDR. He stretched so to see over you, the chair
wobbled
He fired and missed FDR
Hit Cermak, a few others, killed Miss Gill

You reached behind, you hit him, grabbed his arm
As others mobbed the bastard
That chair left toppled, by his gun.

No medals for happenstance

No dinners to commend or statues erected

For just being somewhere, no matter how consequential

But if not for you, would that chair have wobbled, and the bricklayer's

Bullets found their mark

And then what?

ENOUGH ALREADY

Leave us alone, Ok,

With our stubble and razors in mirrored reflections

Of who we are or want to be

Hard enough to peer into aging eyes about what kind of man

we are

In fact,go to hell to the razor company now turned against

our genomic imprints back to Adam,

if there ever was an Adam

You want us to throw off evolution

become a perfectly evolved

Politically aware and correct modern man

For what?

Leave us alone

Equal measures warrior and poet

Tough and gentle

Brawler and lover

Etc …etc..and on and on

We can find our hirer selves ourselves

Sharpen the blade, said Somerset Maugham

In every shave there is a philosophy, a moment to observe

where we are

Each morning, and where we might be headed

Even if it is the same old path
Leave men to their own world, their mini mind outlook,
Their razor's edge

Lather up, cut yourself, find a styptic pencil,
Cover your wounds, but don't cauterize your soul to
Be perfectly correct, speak up and out
The toxicity only rises if you let it,
there is not a damn thing
Wrong with you,
it's a long road from the slime
To the cave,
out of Eden to reality.

SMALL TALK

Sucks up time and intellect
A room full of it, frightens
Warriors, boys, and married men

Banal sentences of platitudes
blather of progeny, flights of overstatements,
of praise for everything, ungrounded,
Nodding heads, tight unnatural smiles, arms crooked statues
Holding drinks or eating smoked something in a napkin

Navigating through the sea of nothingness, by saying
little, agreeing and encouraging endless revelations of others
Dare you venture to other things

Affordable housing, homeless, equality, taxes
You must breath in the fetid aroma of the moment
Or suffer being more than a bore, but a social bore
as well

All talk is small talk,
unnerving,
unsettling, and useless

TENTATIVE

Is for losers….

Tyson hits you with 438 .lbs of force
Joltin' Joe even more. All of their power at once
Always; win or lose

Serena brings it forehand or back. Not always brute force
Some with finesse, never ½ way. There is no activity, job,
hobby or
Relationship that is worth anything if it cannot exert your
full
force.

Focus is prudent, planning needed, skills required,
holding back the dark force of all things

better to
fail after a totally energetic explosion, than to manage for
years
or worse a lifetime, stuck somewhere else, as men die young,
grow old and of no consequence

a life played small, pulling punches all the time, blocking,
ducking, jabbing the challenges

the ring life, all the time
Archie's right hook, Rocky's, the real ones', stamina
Every blow with intention, full power, all in
Nothing held back
tentative can prevail, but what life is that

KINTSUGI

What you do not want broken
breaks
Into pieces some jagged and sharp
And as you reach to retrieve them
Skin is lacerated, blood flows and
Eventually abates

Dinner plates and coffee cups
Windshields cracked by road debris
Dining rooms chairs, expensive children's toys
Grandmother's favorite vase, the stem on that one long rose
You sent her to commemorate some damn event

The Japanese have thought it through, the centuries
that most cracks can be repaired, in pottery, at least
With powdered lacquer of gold, silver and platinum
Taking the shattered and resealing them, with elegant gold
lines, that make the destroyed whole again

Answering the koan
Can what was once whole and admired, be reassembled,even
after it is
shattered ?
Kintsugi is their answer, in a craftsman hand, the parts are
returned to the whole

The wounds healed, gold paste, juxtaposing chunk to chunk,
offering something of more value than the original?

Where is the golden lacquer that can be applied
to shattered dreams, the battlefield dead, and
the women you wanted to stay and are gone

Where is that internal powdered lacquer
to piece together all regrets, foibles, and errors
In a life of regrets.

Blanket in My Sleep

This goes back some years
As a teenage boy, after playing on the narrow black top street
Whatever was in season, often bruised and swollen of eye
or cheek
I would collapse on the living room couch, and fall into the
dreamless
Refuge of utter exhaustion

And I would awake with a blanket over me
Placed there by my mother, at all times of the year
From the chill of a January afternoon, to the humidity of
high noon
in August, blanketed I was

And it followed me,this ritual of some caring soul tossing
that blanket, from Peoria to Manhattan, Boston to Los
Angeles,
15-20 places, children in pairs, through comings and goings,
births and
Inevitable loss

And then still exhausted, there was always a couch,chair
or bed
In some outpost in China, a rustic nook in the Caribbean,
or even the plush spots

from Kona to Vegas

That gesture of kindness, love, and care is long gone

And I long for it now,

as I shiver awake, the blanket on the floor

WHEN WAS THE LAST TIME YOU HEARD FROM GOD

God speaks to Abraham, the angel saves Issac
God tells Moses to take the Israelites to the Promised
Land
He appears in dreams to Solomon and Paul
invades Joseph's thoughts, appears in various guises as a
burning bush, thunder, or hell fire

To Gideon he had the fleece for Saul, a bright light, even
Balaam
Had a donkey
And when the voice grew small for Elijah, it was still there

So to whom does the King of Kings, the exalted Yahweh
speak to now?
Is there some whisper, sign, or cloud from which the word
can emerge?
There is no Ark, no place to address Moses between the
cherubs on its top,
No need to cover our faces, to protect us from the scalding
of our faces as his presence emerges.
No sunburned Moses, stunned by his eminence.

God has just stopped talking and appearing,

out of disgust, or some sense that we

can figure it all out on our own.

Or that Jesus solved it all.

One son,one solution.

or are there just no worthy listeners, who can rise to Elijah,

Moses, Abraham, Sarah or Ruth, none around or yet created.

Mere mortals,all, who might hear him

If we put down our phones. If he appeared in some bush,

who would believe it, anyway

No indication now, there is one universe, instead a vastness

beyond our current brains, simpletons we are to grasp it.

We are alone in this one, perhaps, without this one know it

all presence, of a God, who has stopped talking

To a species evolved, confused, to find all answers and

direction on our own.

Perhaps a whisper to someone,

or a natural sign that we are heading in the right

direction, or will we even survive.

Are faith, prayer and belief enough

for a sound out of the darkness

RUNNING AGROUND

There was a track a click or two from Madame Mu's
Deep inside the 5th ring
By the teacher's college in mid – August yellow smog
I thought I would be alone
All eight lanes were full, three inner lanes for actual runners
Like me, and then a menagerie of Chinese, some with swords
Teenage girls in short skirts, old men and women in street
clothes
All out at dawn, given access by a young, uniformed man
with
A black, submachine gun

Out of the safety of a kibbutz near the Golan Heights, I
ran with
IDF soldiers, all in khaki shorts, bare chested, and in boots,
laughing
At how slow I am, as we passed their tanks, artillery, armored
personnel
Carriers
As the run ended, they had me lift shells into a truck, then
fed me

Safer around soldiers and Uzi's than on a night jaunt around
Central Park

Down by the turn past 102nd, or anytime on Belle Island outside Detroit, or
Off the Mall in DC

Running releases you for the time it takes to go from here to there, from
Whatever cloud that has enveloped you, or let's you think it through
But what explanation works or fits how obsessive it becomes
How can you explain marathons, run over and again, in New York,
Boston, Honolulu, LA until you get to 25,
Twenty Four hour attempts around a high school track, or 100 k
From the Liberty Bell to the Boardwalk in Atlantic City
For what reason, who can be sure

Trek through Death Valley just to meet a long lost friend, who misses
the starting line the next year, seized by a soft organ cancer

Perhaps,it is just to say I AM here and still around
And no matter how life goes, I will never run
Aground

THEY EAT OYSTERS AT XMAS

Poetry written in winter is sadder than in Spring
Old injuries hurt more
A chill comes and does not leave
Bone deep doubts
Linger and then consume the psyche
No one smiles much and certainly not at you

Everything shortens
Your hamstrings and Achilles
And condenses
Daylight, energy, time outside
Forced inside to roam within your
Clutter and aged things, of no meaning

And gaiety is far away
In Paris they eat oysters at Xmas
Couples do turns on ice by the Eiffel Tower
Ponies are circling a small path through a dusting of snow
As children in berets laugh

From a 5 .lb box of chocolates, you can savor a few, suck
on them

Close your eyes, hoping to open them to a fireplace in a
warm cabin
Lights on a fresh tree, and the soft sound of snow piling up
on roof

And maybe a plate of oysters.

AND 19 YEARS LATER HE DIED

Soup cans, and Coca Cola logos
Monroe and celebrities en masse
Foil covered silver painted walls covered his studio cum
party mecca

They all came
politician, musician, a clique of the self styled, preening
creative people of the time.
Names aglow as their painted faces and tattooed asses
Ultra Violet, Nico, Candy Darling, and, of course, Viva
All to rub against Andy, who had a soft spot for hangers on
and freaks

Even the President of a one person society that called for
the outright
Elimination of all men
Valerie,it was who ran the Society for Cutting up Men
(SCUM),
Solanas who wanted him to produce her play about it all
UP YOUR ASS

Warhol gets more fame, moves his Factory to 33 Union
Square West and has forgotten Val and her SCUM,play
and all.

Somebody to Nobody," leave me the hell alone", he might have said, but

did not.

Solanas fumes in her single room, her paranoia raging that he has stolen her precious play

delusions put a .32 Beretta in one hand and a .22 in the other. 3 June 1968, she walks into his new place and plugs Andy and London gallery owner, Mario Amaya. Amaya is grazed. Warhol has his guts torn apart. Stomach and liver. Spleen and Esophagus. And then both lungs hit

He was dead.

Then he came back,

two months to recuperate and heal, and a lifetime in a corset to hold what was left of his guts in place.

Solanas gets three years. Yeah. Three years.

Spends the next 20 years in a SRO in San Francisco as paranoid as ever, hoping for SCUM to become real.

Dies alone.

June was a bad time for most of America '68

Just two days after Andy gets it, Bobby is in the hands of busboy, Juan Romero, bleeding out, as a crowd screams and Rosie Grier breaks Sirhan's thumb.

Martin, Bobby, and Warhol nearly.

Afraid of doctors, guns, and most people

Warhol retreats into

That caged existence that comes from a terror that runs to some dark place no one but you can find

Whatever horror the fear of death might have held for him was multiplied by the moments the spinning metal pierced him.

It was the gall bladder surgery, he delayed for years that brought on the cardiac arrest

killed him that February in 1987, not the bullets.

More so the fear of men in white coats and antiseptic hospitals, with nothing on the walls but paint.

A legacy of fine art,

the inventor of pop,

lost to a paranoid clown, who wanted all men dead,

but got just one

19 years after she fired the shot.

Up Your Ass, Valerie.

CLIMATE CHANGE

I know they all say its warmer

It rains torrents and tornadoes are all level 5's

Snow is deeper, the jet stream is out of place

San Diego and Manhattan are all about to sink

All that coal is vile and the Permian basin with its oil and
gas is a loss

And no one gives a good god damn who loses what job as
long as

The climate change stops, or at least it abates a degree or two

Damned we all are

Who drive Henry Ford gas turbine engines

Who do not flock to sit outside a 7/11 and charge our Volts
and fancy cars

By the homeless guys shuffling for a buck to buy a crappy
burrito

Anyone caught on the grid with coal power, maybe fined,
damned or

incarcerated, while they let out the real crooks, thieves,

a few violent sexual offenders

Is it really warmer now

Than the time the dinosaurs roamed for a few hundred
million

years, farting

leaving tons of crap and methane gas until that comet came along.

Ice ages came and went, the Riss, Mindel, Wurm

And some say we are at the end of the Pleistocene,the warm between the next ice age return

Agree that it's the CO_2, but maybe the sun plays a bigger role and there's not

a damn thing we can do about that.

That sun just gets bigger anyway and will become a Red Giant, as it ages.

So what is the rush?

A degree or so warmer and it happens sooner, more like Mars, in a few billion years.

Is that what is on us, really, when you say, OK Boomer

When the whining stops, perhaps you can hear the answers that

do not line the pockets of smart asses,who took our money as subsidies and ran to the bank, to sell 357,000 EV cars

7 damn % of all cars

Fusion, new nuke plants, quantum computers to figure it out.

Try all of that, before I give up my 1968 GTO or my Ford truck.

DOES THE PELICAN KNOW

As it glides over the bay
Water still and clear enough to see some fish there
of some type it can spear and swallow to survive
That it will most likely fail

It is not trial and error
There are no corrections to be made
Some imbedded DNA directs an endless
Flight path over bay and sea

Observed as beautiful and an aerial ballet
It is for the pelican the way of things
An avian Sisyphus
Resting on a lone buoy, the launching pad of another
mission, to find the elusive, but required prey
To live, and soar again

And most do,without squawk, go
Into the wind, until that moment when they dive
Unexpected, mostly to emerge wet, with nothing in their
beaks
or bellies
Like the more sentient of us
Rising from our buoy, the bed to soar in auto and plane
To snap something from the waters we penetrate to return with

some morsel of sustenance

Knowing that it is nothing much
but enough
to coax us back again and again
for small rewards
In a life of small returns

The pelican flies but cannot know
The outcome, so it flies again
Why do we ?

THE TALE OF THE TWO TORTOISE

Darwin thought it wise to spend his time on islands
Writing notes about creatures who swim, crawl, and fly
Surmising in his mind's eye that they were connected
One leading to another linked as time passed into a progression
Or evolution, most dying away and only the strong surviving

This before CRISPR, DNA, any understanding of telomeres, genomes, or
epigenetics. Observations, copulating, and propagation everywhere on Galapagos
humping birds, reptiles, and mammals
erections into holes, yielding a progeny that sustained and evolved species

Diego the tortoise is Darwinian
This aggressive male fights his way to mount
Every shell he can find, ready or not
To receive his reptilian probe
And the receiver must open her portal to accommodate
The size of him and receive the seed
Which he,they say, has deposited hundreds of times
And now is the father of over 800

A one turtle, survival game to repopulate his niche in
The evolutionary cycle
All push and shove
It in that is

More than one, screws in a different way
With less bravado

Roaming in a quiet way
Nuzzling and preening from shell to female shell
GT 5 found his way into more
Orifices
Thrusting his way to a brood of over 1,000 or so
Slowly doing the up and back for twenty minutes at a time
Adding his moaning to the symphony of mating sounds
Perhaps not as fit, or aggressive, but progressive enough

Both retired now to the wild
Away from captivity
Each over 100, rolling out their phallus
From shell to shell
Until they cannot until the last day
Both survivors and fit enough, each in their own way

PREP H ON THE TOOTHBRUSH

Sun rises over the mountains, snow capped
Just beyond the Vegas strip
Distracted by a quiet night at a blackjack table
The toothbrush that I am running over my gums
Has an odd smell and taste
I brush the caps, bridges, and root canals
50 grand of work over the recent years
Mostly paid for by being here
shuffling cards,
Chips and cash, as a side hustle

I spit the brew out
And see the tube of Prep H nearby and the Crest far away
I manage a crooked cowboy smile
Pleased that I did not shove the toothpaste up my ass
But not celebrating that much
realizing how there was not much room for
anything with my head so firmly placed there anyway

The mirror reflects back its own philosophy
It sees what is, if you but face it squarely.
Each line a highway on the journey of a curved life
Few straightaways, and when they came, no trooper to slow
you down

A scar for when you fell as boy, another from a bullies right hook,
and gully of a frown, by the corner of your mouth
from seeing the world to seriously,
always

Lather up
The path to salvation is hard said that Katha Upanishad
From the ancients, common thoughts really, not esoteric
And we are all, men, on the edge hoping to not be
Cleaved, or have our balls cut off
As we maneuver through it
Each morning shaving off the stubble of before
As though all the coarseness of the last day can be scrapped away
In the warm spray of the faucet and the slide of the blade

Everyday a chance for another crawl across the edge of the life knife
A new philosophy to be tried or an old one to be obeyed
And a chance to choose the Prep H or the Crest
If you are awake enough to choose wisely

IT IS NEVER THE BIG STUFF

That makes you change
If you ever do
Away from your nature
And acquired notions
Of what is best for you
All that you think you know
Of how to act and be
Until clarity hits you in the face
With a 2 x 4

Accumulate misgivings
Of women come and gone
Wrong things said at work
Good deeds pissed upon
Turns you could have taken
Bosses you should not have cursed and
Scorned
Risks that were better taken and others frowned
Upon
More attention to the future and less time wasted
here and now

Ambition pursued and not abhorred
Showing up when truly needed not just when

Time allowed

And being calm and certain,

Learning when to cave on some project of some other

That you could not embrace

No one is screaming any longer

Or watching your every move

Not a single soul out to get you

No need since everyone knows

only

You are out to get you

Affront or indiscretion

Misstep or humiliation, bad manners

Or poor taste

Just one, at the wrong time after a lifetime of misgivings

Busted dreams, no dreams, and a few nightmares,

Few prospects ahead, and a longing to actually be dead

She comes asking for a buck

That letter you want to send is personal

Not business, she asks.

"Yeah, its personal"

"then you need to pay for postage"

"you came all this way for that"

"sure, just give me a dollar"

A handful of nickels and dimes
A deep breath
that inaudible curse
and you promise yourself that's it
the final indignity and you'll walk out
into that cold parking lot, turn the key
and be gone.

Maybe someday
Another indignity, embarrassment or small thing will
End it. It will.

LOST IN NAIROBI

There are few dreams remembered

Most lost as consciousness returns,

Standard models of running in place, going through tunnels,

Naked appearances

Who interprets dreams in the modern era

Where Freud has left us with the unconscious mind, and our

Id's and Ego's and sexual repressions

Who now is the oneirocritic

We are on our own against vivid recollections

That reveal nothing more than the idiosyncratic neural firings

Of our dendrites

So there I am in a small, dirty hotel room

In Narobi, the wind comes through an open window

The street noise is of trucks and buses and a woman's

Voice yells, "wait"

On the bed there are torn pieces of a map of Kenya

And I am frantic, attempting to put them together

A tall slim African woman arrives and puts together the map, she has

Blood on her hands

She takes off her clothes

Puts her hands on my throat and begins to strangle me

I cannot shake her as she smiles serenely
As the driver of the bus yells
"Come on, I can't wait any longer"

And I awaken
Go to the sink in the room
As though it was all a dream
I look at my tongue it is covered in blood
And the wash basin is filled with dark, almost purple blood
And I scream
Grow silent

And awake where I am, at the typewriter, wet with sweat
Like it is August in Philadelphia
Except its January

I am Glad I Danced with You

That night under the crystal chandeliers
Where we could see the city below us through windows
Ceiling to floor, clear through to the George Washington
Bridge
And a line of red lights of harried commuters racing north
out of town

Some forgotten event in that Rainbow Room where
slow dances still were played and
men and women could sway,
rub against each other,
touch cheeks and speak softly

Offering some thought as a gesture,
urbane and sophisticated,
suggesting a coarser coupling perhaps, never promised, if
expected,
when the music ended

memory cannot recall
the small talk, the band, menu or companions
only you
of long neck, and pearls,

perfume that was a scent through many years
remembered from pillow to stove
and the grace across a polished, wooden, floor
allowing me to believe for that night I could dance
if barely
That place faded like all rainbows
was renovated
Shut down during a recession
paid off the mob to handle union types
never to be a place where regular folks
could rub leg and hip together
whisper into each others ears,
about what might happen next

And I've given up the ruse
That I could move across the parquet
Without you
To dance no more
Bite a diamond studded ear
Or pretend that we would dance like that forever
As the commuters headed towards home over the GW
bridge.

IN THE PRESENCE OF ASSHOLES

Somewhere you will find one
they are not hard to see across any parking lot
or just ordering at KFC
Doing what they want and wish for no one else to see
So self involved they are to not include you or me

It's the guy from some South Asian island with a handful
of Lotto numbers
the numbers are all losers anyway, but he must watch over
each one,
and then just
When you hope he is done, as you stand there with your
frozen mini pizza,
He orders games from under the glass at 7/ 11.
And the guy behind the counter
In his Sikh turban, is about to reach for his kirpan.

Then, you get behind another asshole at the dry cleaner, who
must count out
50 of his shirts. 50.
One by one, as he determines the color, stripe and hue, and
separates them,
even though Alex tells him it does not matter.
Then he folds them.

An asshole with ADD or on the autism spectrum .

A large man with tattoos across his face, and a snake in red and black on his left

arm, quietly coaxes the man to finish.

The guy tells him to fuck off.

And the snake armed guy, walks out, lights up a Camel. And the asshole keeps folding.

I chat up the displaced tattooed man, who says quietly,

"he is not worth it man"

You find wisdom everywhere

Often elicited after a run in with any asshole

They are the invaders, the Area 51 arrivals,

Aliens they are, they cannot be like the rest of us

Some twisted umbilical cord, a lack of oxygen at birth,

A mangled childhood that suggested to these entitled

Self centered, miscreants that the world as

they see it

is the world.

Watch out for them

Be on the lookout

There may be more of them than us eventually

Until I figure it out, I will adopt the view of

Taz, the tattooed man

"He ain't worth it man"

THE BEGGAR'S COAT

Do you wear it?
the beggar's coat
Like Bartimaeus the blind one
Who was by roadside when Jesus came by
Asked to be healed and then was by
Christ or so it says in Mark 10:46-52

Was it not that Jesus could heal him
As much as he had faith that he would
No Longer need that coat, they all wore, the blind ones then
To signify they could not see
he threw it away, and walked towards the voice of Christ
knowing that he would be healed
So sure he was that the beggar's coat was who he was
not who he would become

Do we all wear that coat that proclaims who we are
What path we have chosen and are so intent to remain upon
Are we so bound by our present circumstances that we
cannot shed the past
And walk away from the tattered, soiled, cloak that identifies
us now

We are not blind, or infirm
except burdened by a colossal lack of faith in ourselves and
some higher power
Have we no belief in destiny or even a simple surprise that
life might
Reveal to us, if we but let it

It is the coat of the beggar, signifying a victim of circumstance
and happenstance
Not of victory, adventure
a belief if not in others, but only ourselves
Throw it away, pile them high, collect those of other men,
and set fire to
Them, all of them,

Shower,shave, be renewed, identified only
by your dreams and grit!

In the Village there is a Woman

There is a place the Dutch called Groenwijck
In lower Manhattan,
It is still green, has some trees and
Patches of grass
With row houses and old condos
Where the Bohemians lived once
More eclectic now, with career women sharing rooms
Gay men often walking dogs, big and small, as the men
stroll arm in arm
And everyone else attracted to bars and restaurants with
open gardens
In backyards you cannot see
Lights always on somewhere, and a band playing jazz 'til 4 am

Greenwich Village, of course, it is

I knew a woman there, who had a quiet place
A huge bed, small dog and a fat, serene cat, and a real fireplace
That she had me ply with pine logs in winter, as I stood
naked, covered
by a black robe
On Minetta Street, she lived, that sat atop a long ago buried
brook,

Called 'devil water' in Tammany Hall days

Short black hair, sturdy frame, and
colossal essential parts front and behind
that she put to use in exotic ways, unmoored by standard
approaches to pleasure, orgasm frequency, or convention

what happened there seemed fitting
in a bed over a 'devil water' brook
launching fluids all over the place from fireplace to table top
and then sucked into
the warm grip of her birth canal

The only respite
an evening walk to a spot
Named in Longfellow's poem, imagined, perhaps from
Revere's ride
One if by Land, Two if by Sea
To a table she always had reserved,far back by a window
Where between courses she had my hand between her legs
I was on fire by the time we returned to her fireplace
where we roared through the night, until the fire was embers
at daybreak

How I ever left the village that winter to do anything else
Still confounds
But even the best of it, gets old after a time,
Or more likely …..she tired of me

WHAT DO YOU BELIEVE

There is not much talk about it
Longshoremen and fork lifters
Long haul drivers and men walking steel beams
Even tooth drillers and the proctologist
Do not just volunteer what they believe

Some say they have no religion
Formally
When pressed they say they believe in God
For some it is the standby, Jesus Christ
some admit to church or temple
but relatively few
others have some uncertainty about their point of view

more and more are doubters about the guiding presence of
some unknowable force
agnostic, if they knew the term
while atheists are certain and do not doubt their claim
that there is nothing but ourselves to ever blame

every religion has its own leap of faith to some
tale or tome, that no logic would allow, founding stories of
Joseph Campbell
fame, one as lame as any other, and
in some ways all the same

Sumerians had Gilgamesh, Christians have their Christ,
Jews the fable of Moses, Mormons, Joseph Smith and his
tablets of gold,
Each borrowed from another, Gabriel was busy, as was
Elijah, even Mohammed
ascended to Allah meeting all the above, along the way
Each their own version of what to do and say
To reach heaven, nirvana, or live a righteous life

And those most devout often seem no more
a better person, kind or forgiving except in church that day
And the true believers took up arms to murder and protect
less
Celestial concerns.
Men of belief did impose an Inquisition, torture and convert,
Crusade for Christ and murder Jews along the way
Muslim caliphates subjugated millions, Hindu mobs still
impose horror
In India's villages,
segregation, false imprisonment, banishment, and prejudice
still reign
all under the eyes of that force larger than ourselves

So is it any wonder that fewer still believe
That there is a higher essence directing all our paths
Christ will save us, ultimately and come back to eradicate
the past

The Talmud if followed after reading for seven and a half years

Would set a clear direction

Quran read and memorized, delivered to the Prophet over 23 years

Still revered

Yet for every adherent, there are fewer the polls all say

More who decline to say what they believe

And

Perhaps it would be enough if everyone on the planet just believed

That to do unto others as you would have them do to you

Would offer what we all need

Right and that will happen, when ?

SOLITARY

Deep within there is chill
That I cannot shake away
It runs through me even
On the hot and humid days

the bones are cold and my mind in
cold storage, waiting for a thaw
but it is not the weather that brings it on
it is that there are no warm bodies to touch
or huddle near, no voices in the dark to render
comfort near

totally and undeniably alone
has its virtues
quiet when you need it
no schedules to obey
eat what the hell you want on any given day
sing a tune you can remember, scream at the bastard next
door
cry over a rose or poem
listen to Gershwin, again
read about Cyrus, Lenin, and Elvis in one afternoon
run through the desert when its 103 at high noon
and eat a piece of fruit once in awhile

Yet

I am in solitary
of my making,incarcerated on my own
singularity my reality, turning towards whatever
moved me, and away from everything and everyone else
to this confinement,uncaged, and un cuffed
to a cell alone, cut off by temperament and lost desire
of all that once compelled
now hollowed out, from a life once richer, textured with
other souls,
the pain of it not enough to change and that
chill bearable and benign
until the fire comes.

THE TROLLS RULE

There are trolls everywhere

On line somewhere ripping apart

Whoever they wish, so they can hurt and savage

The powerful, the weak, the different,

or that neighborhood kid who excels at science, the plump girl

In Midsummer Nights' Dream, the cancer survivor who lost her breasts

They do not care

These sadists, narcissists, in need of therapy

Socio and psychopaths

They know how to make people suffer

And they revel in it

When they hurt you, they celebrate

So happy they are that they are now important

Self righteous, usually anonymous, attacking to

prove to themselves they exist

There were always trolls

They whispered in cliques

Told lies about you

Worked hard to break up your life

Because it was wholesome which the troll

Could not stand

And when you found them out, you would call them out

Break a nose, open a lip, or bang their head against a red brick wall

In the school yard, until their face was purple and red

There were less trolls then

Now they want to rule any good person or deed

destroy so they can feed their personality disorder

They are turning us all into victims, weepers, and

A nation fearful of saying anything for fear you will

Be trolled

They orient their lives around attention

Not accomplishment

They despise values that suggest caring, helping and triumph over adversity

There is no electronic equivalent of a school yard beat down

No way to put a slug into their skulls

Only to go on

Write, achieve, and touch

In any way you can or must

And if you do come across one

Hit them square in the face

For me

OK.

BEACH CLEANER

Before dawn there is not much too see
On the bay
Two old dogs chasing each other as their owner buries her
head in her phone
Conversing with who can imagine about what at 5:30
The homeless, Matthew pulls up his blanket and strikes a
fetal pose on his
concrete bench,
Seth and Marigold sitting on the sand
stare into the still dark landscape as though a signal from
God will come to them
that morning ending the lunacy that is their lives

in the distance,

a yellow bulldozer lumbers from blue trash can to blue
trashcan
there on its front blade, stands Shaq, with the proud look of
a man heading some
grand parade, on a mission to save someone or something
he jumps off the dozer blade with vigor, puts his large white
gloves around the cans and lifts them,
dumping the content into the dozer scooper

he unloads three of them, he walks the beach and picks up
diapers, bras, and
butts, into a separate bag, and tosses it into the scooper and
signals
Lionel
"take it up, take it up, Lionel"

Maybe 100 barrels on this stretch, no stopping these two
save for the occasional water, from a fountain for people
that people let
Their Yappies drink from .

Slowly he takes off his gloves, then his hat, massages his
bald head
And drinks, long and slow
Reverses the ritual
climbs back on the blade and motions his right hand forward
like a commander of
a tank brigade

Continuing on unnoticed

For as far as there are cans of trash, bags from Chick Fil A,
crap in the sand,
Vodka bottles
Shaq and Lionel out there cleaning up for the rest of us

Before the sun breaks over the mountains
Without complaint or whine
Old fashioned men, and a bulldozer doing a job for a few bucks
And a small degree of satisfaction.

OPERATOR 51
WHERE ARE YOU

Once there were women who typed and took phone calls
Some ran the offices of men of power
Organized their days, directed their bosses life, and often
Covered for all mistakes and dalliances
Sorted out calendar and appointments and had
Secret numbers to call, when he wanted to be unreachable

But if you were important enough, vital in most things, you couldn't ever be
Not available, ever
So they fixed that, one executive did, after finding a VP, shacked up with his gal,
responsible for having his secret number, she did, but, she was with him that
afternoon, when Chairman So and So, wanted to sign somebody to a long term
deal, that would save 'prime time'

He set up Operator 51,
who had the numbers and locations of everyone,
and you would call her, and she would find the guy, and connect you immediately.

She knew where you were, and often, who you might be
with from family to wayward co- worker,
she never told anyone.
No event was ever too large or small,
she would find you,
you were never out of reach of some higher up who just had
to "God damn it, find
him" on his lips

Three Mile Island is about to level Pennsylvania,
Pope John Paul dies in 33 days after elected,
John Lennon is murdered outside the Dakota

All went through Operator 51, she found me changing oil,
cutting grass, or attempting to be a father to the children,
others had boundaries, imposed by phones, and beepers
No ubiquitous information stream staring out of every
nearby screen
Invading any sense of private space, or time away
Now no fences at all, to keep you away, out of the fray, or
anyone from
getting to you all the time, from trivial to majestic,
Austere to grandiose
All on display, no operator required to find you
And you are likely to always be indisposed
Nostalgia overtakes me, when a particularly gnarly text calls me
Out for some perceived indiscretion
"How the hell could you let that happen"
Operator 51, where are you?

THEY ARE DYING ON EVEREST

Rich men and women climb
The highest mountain mostly
They hire guides with permits that take them up
Paths well known and traveled, soiled
By human waste, and littered with the junk of
oxygen bottles, and high energy snack wrappers
From summit to the base

Hilary and Norgay did not summit without help
They were not alone
400 on the expedition, 362 porters, 20 Sherpa,
10,000 pounds of baggage
For 15 minutes on the summit
A snapshot of Norgay, none of Hilary
They were alone at the rooftop of the world
And they lived to tell the tale and more

Dying now these adventure junkies
So intent on marking it off their bucket list
Created out of opulence and personal
Aggrandizement, long ago not on the world's list
Of things that must be explored,examined, invented,
Made right or advanced.
Just having the interest, the desire, the cash to do it

So do it.

No matter the danger ahead for others, the pursuit of danger

As though it actually fulfills some need beside, I can.

There is a line, in May, on the edge of the mountain, a narrow edge, that

Hilary and Norgay could walk, discover the Hilary Step, and summit.

Along that path today, there are huddled climbers in parkas, filled with space age

Insulation, and oxygen bottles, that allows them to sit and wait, in a

Traffic jam of wannabes for two hours up, and a wait at the summit of two more

Hilary and Norgay spent 15 minutes there and it was enough to

Tell the world we have done something special here

Too many dead on Everest

To complete a climb for what, other than

So you can find yourself, challenge your mettle, proof you are

The more frightening journey

Is the Everest of your soul, the inner journey

That one without oxygen or crampons is as daunting as any other

And the results are longer lasting, and often as harrowing

The most terrifying climb is the inner journey. And it is uncharted and there is no waiting

I Got the Impeachment Blues

They are not chiseled into a mountain side
Hardly remembered although once all the rage
Presidents who erred along the way
Cleveland and his bastard child
Johnson impeached in 68, 11 articles in all
For firing his secretary of war
Edwin Stanton forgotten overtime and Johnson as well
Clinton impeached on charges he lied to a federal grand jury
And then obstructed justice, all over an affair with a brunette
Named Monica

Neither were removed from office
And the country moved along, no one constitutionally
concerned that
The Republic would fall or fail

A flashy, brash, outlier gets to be President
The opposition would dissent, moan that is evil incarnate
For a mouthy developer to be President, and years later
They find a Trump hater emerges with a claim that this
POTUS
withheld funds from the Ukraine to have them find dirt
On old Joe .

They impeach on two counts for abusing his power and obstruction,
And the Senate pledges a trial
And both sides claim the people know what is right, and their votes may
ultimately decide

But all this jabber over impeachment may seem to them compelling
While it has just given the 'people'

The impeachment blues

Some complain of the rain, the incessant cold and snow
The car that will not turn over, getting the school lunches ready,
Finding enough cash to pay for a root canal, get your man bun companion to
Give you enough covers to keep you warm
Why aunt Sally refuses to eat sushi on every Friday night
How Don and David refuse to drink your Russian vodka because the taste
Is so vile, or why Raul prefers Andrea and not Marcia, with the lips and green eyes

Or how can that couple from Ohio find a 500 square foot room for less than
1700 a month

The cable guys hammer us with the news. Impeachment is here, the sky is falling.
Chicken littles of digital journalism, hoping to generate enough sound to
overcome the day to day, hum and drum.

Its blue enough, the mood, no enhancement needed, Wolf, and Todd

The morose, mundane, ebb and flow of life, under a winter sky, but, far from the
Darkness at noon, that cloud they have painted over the White House
Awaiting solemn oaths and testimony to prove that politics rules, even if it will
Likely be forgotten, fade like other historical notes, have another election,
And wonder only if there is enough money to rent, eat, and buy enough gas to get
away from it all

And who is whistling the impeachment blues, outside the beltway

Not a soul

WHAT ALL THE OLD DAMES WANT

There are no dames anymore
They faded away after the big war
The stuff of Rogers and Hammerstein revivals
No more washing men out of your hair
Impolitic to claim that there is nothing like a dame

Now modern women all claim they are not anywhere the
same
Unique individuals each one with desires and needs as
different as
The snowflakes they caught on their tongues before puberty
and hot
flashes

More of them unmoored from any one man
One in two separated or divorced, prospecting for that
golden man
Who is 18k, finding mostly men who turn as green as their
cheap wedding bands
Who are going to take them to dinner and
hope for a screw and little else

They ride the dating sites after the same man, all of them

He must have humor or a sense of it, be witty, and smart
Be clean and neat with face hair or not, love travel, and be fit enough to
not scare her when undressed, have wide interests that coincide with hers,
Be attentive and warm, be friendly and outgoing, and always be a good friend
Not just to her, but her friends as well,
Be a good companion,
Carry on a conversation with family and friends
And most want you to love animals, especially dogs
Or on occasion a cat
And then there is be a food lover, a gourmand,
Who likes to cook or at least appreciates women who do
But not demand it, or expect it, but only enjoy it when offered
Other than that, no problem

There may be a dame or two left out there in cyberspace
On some dating site, who just wants a regular guy, who wants someone to
Listen to him, bring a smile to his lips, and screw him until morning

If so swipe right, or left or whatever

WHO KILLED WU HUAYAN

It is not easy to survive in Guizhou
A small town in the China behemoth that
does not reach the people there
Poverty still has a grip on this myth of the grand Chinese
economic monolith
Neither Mao nor Xi Jinping have figured out how to give
their people anything
to sustain them except little red books and thought control

Ms. Wu was 24, in college
Gave up her food rations to pay off
Her brothers medical bills
Ate only some rice and chili peppers
And some days ate one steamed bun
Left her malnourished
4 feet, five inches
And weighed 47.3 pounds

She made her way to a hospital
And her friends raised funds on
Shuidichou, 30 thousand to be exact
No matter how much she suffered the
hospital only accounted for 3,000 of it
The rest went into the pockets of her

providers

Modern China unchanged, generations of corruption

From the Manchu to today

Content to let her waste away

From her bed, in cute fuzzy, blue pajamas

She offered thanks

Only to die days later of heart and kidney diseases

And they held a quiet memorial service at

Guizhou Forerunner College

Ms. Wu

murdered by a system that did not see her or want to

who imagined the Long March would lead to this

It Gets So Dark
There is No Light

At the end of that tunnel, is there?

Bills are piled Denali high
The credit cards debt is overextended
Amex is calling to cut a deal
The second mortgage is over 90 grand
And there are no helping hands
Parents are dead, your sister is raising her daughter alone
And your friends, are good for solace but not cash

Everyone says live the life you want
Do what gives you life and fills you up
Take a risk, get out of that rutted life
Be alive, chart a course on the edge
Don't look back,
God wants you to be prosperous

Follow your bliss, Campbell famously remarked

But I might have looked ahead
Looked down at the holes in the road
Contemplated the consequences of my actions
Intended that I could see and the unintended
That I could not

Darkest December morning
Driving into a deserted downtown
Up 30 floors to a see a man, awake and working in a white
shirt and Xmas tie
At 5:45

Dressed in my best suit and sharpest two tone, cuff linked
shirt, I amuse the
man, trying to convince him and me, I am not about to step
onto the gallows
of bankruptcy
He assures me it will be best and in five years or so, I will
be fine
without a house, credit, or my debt
but quite able to go on

30 floors later
In the meat locker garage
I am sweating, my French cuff shirt soaked
By the time I turn on the heat, strip down, and
Put on a black T shirt
I rip up the papers and decide to just
Drive as fast as I can through that tunnel,
Until I see the light again, it must be there,right ?

DEMIMONDE

Everyone is so proper

And correct politically they say

All in line, now, no one allowed to be out of society

Norms

You cannot utter new and not mean old

Say gal or,God forbid, broad in anyway to anyone

You cannot dare touch even someone you may know

or embrace, in any way, unless it is man to man which seems

Ok.

And any coarse words are considered more than merely

risqué

Unless uttered by a woman, upset about anything, even not

getting her latte

properly served at Starbucks

Seriousity rules, no gaiety allowed

Moulin Rouge and Folies Bergere outlawed today

No Toulouse –Lautrec hanging out

garters and the Can- Can banished

In the actual world

while on their phone apps

Teenager girls give blow jobs

And young men get drunk and wasted

While Mom is lost on oxy and cousin Brian dies of fentanyl

Because the cop who finds him, is out of narcan

Le Demi- monde, that half world created by Dumas
as a comedy, opened the way to the nether world of drugs
Drinking, gambling
The high life for flaneurs, who walked the boulevards
buying, whatever was their fancy from fashion to whores

Hedonism had a place
Demimondaine's had respect and played courtesan to
royals and
commoners with equal vigor
Then came the war, suffrage, prohibition, the repeal,
another war
The fight against communism, for civil rights, equality, and
just holding onto
that rung on the ladder that was between you and the abyss

No time for debauchery
sleep, let alone the pursuit of pleasure
cannot be accused of being part of the demimonde
It is all too serious, prescribed, sensitive
And dangerous, to live outside or below the line.

THE VIEW FROM CRYSTAL PIER

Waves at 5 feet, well formed below
Emerald green and clear the ocean reflects the
Early morning sun, with golden shimmer into
The dark eyes of the fisherman at piers end
Needing a catch to overcome a long nights fast
Sleeping under the pylons

Out past the break the surfers paddle
Men in black suits on brightly colored boards
Spaced far apart, serious about their Zen
The essential imposed solitude of the morning
Wave catchers, the unspoken code
'let me be,man, just me and the wave'

One outlier appears
A woman paddles out in a two piece bikini
Dazzling in her nudity surrounded by men in black
Her legs bent at the knees, and her long arms pulling her out
No one stops or turns, she is just another devotee
of the morning routine
But then she paddles to that first wave and takes it with
sharp turns and speed
that strong body admirable and classically beautiful

A loud cry is heard from a surfer in the interval between
swells
And they all look
Along the line
She smiles, perhaps, not at them, but, just because here she
is free and strong, and alive with no other bullshit to
handle, but the next wave

The fisherman cursed,
until that fish arrived at hooks end
And I thought it would not
be too bad a day
that began like this

CRACK IN THE SIDEWALK

Crack in the sidewalk

I did not see

Running to that studio I live in by the sea

Not night or dawn or sunset

Daylight

Mind lost in revere of what I might still be

Big thoughts of a future play

Some new cards and a beginning

Getting a new hand for a change of

Everything

A second passes

A toe not lifted catches a barely raised

Concrete slab

Everything ends as you fall

On elbow and knee knowing you cannot stop it at all

And brow bounces on the concrete and bleeds onto

everything

The crash clears the mind

All thoughts obliterated by a wayward step

And you lay there and assess if you can move

You are alone on the ground and it is as quiet

as you imagine death to be

Scared you rise, squeeze the blood out of every wound
Hobble away

The eternal lesson is it not
All is chaos or destiny take your pick
Meant to be or pure chance
Either way, that big dream, that grandiose plan
Gets obliterated in a nanosecond on a sidewalk 500 feet
from that
Lousy studio,you call home

Clean the wounds and be grateful, man,
There is still a face in your mirror

THE GOSPEL ACCORDING TO THE SANCTIFIED THEOMORPHIC OPERATOR

A robot quotes Matthew

offering bible phrases to the old and the lame

Where a pastor might have stood, no longer

SanTo,the machine, with an artificial intelligence does it

No flesh and bone required

A standin Pope may come along the way

White smoke an anachronism finally

Martin Luther might take back his 95 thesis

Rip them off the door at old Wittenberg Castle Church

If knew that Bless U – 2, was commemorating the 500th

Year of that Reformation, spewing blessings to 10,000 believers

From a plastic mouth

And what suffering would Siddhartha Gautama endure

Along the way to Nirvana, if he saw Mindar, an android priest

Lead the prayers for thousands of devotees

Not fully machine learned yet, but far enough along to gesture, move his

Mouth slowly and suggest a placid state of mind, in a truly pure, no mind,
Mushin

No thoughts,
no emotion,
no precepts or concepts,
no ambition,
no fears
No beliefs,
just nothing,

transcendent over consciousness, not difficult for the android, the figurines with artificial intelligence,
harder for humans

and you wonder, if the robots can provide the text, and they can fake empathy
how far away are they anyway from the real, flesh and blood, spiritual guides
who feign connection to the higher power and you and me

2.5 billion Christians, 1.5 billion Muslims, 1.1 billion Hindus
And an army of righteous robots to spread the word
That's the Brave New World
Where is Father O' Brien when we need him?

SELLING CANDY

He is out of place in this tony outdoor mall
In always upscale La Jolla
Jews couldn't live here until 1965
And teenage black boys never ventured here
But here was James going from car to car
With a box of candies, large bars, theater size
Hoping to raise some bucks to show his boss
Who dropped him here to sell candy for some damn cause
or scam

People coming out of that South African dentist office
Who pulled their molars for the cost of a down payment
on their
Benz
Tacos, supersized,are inhaled by three Spanish speaking
landscape guys
A shirt and tie guy exits the Massage Master storefront, with
the covered
windows, with a smile as big as his happy ending

Women in short shorts, make their way to the Vietnamese
nail parlor, and their
eyes never see James or his candy, so intent they are to talk
to their phones

One older woman, bent over and small exits the CVS and
gives him a few bucks
and carries away a monstrous Snickers bar

James is quiet when I ask about the charity, but, he is just a
kid looking to get
some extra cash, and keep his older brother off his back, I
imagine
I pull out a five and give it to him
take no candy. He smiles
And all the separation between him and this place and these
people, fades
"Keep at it James, you'll make it big"
What that meant, he knew
even if I didn't

THAT NIGHT IN PALM SPRINGS

Was a twilight dream
So weird and mainly bizarre
Where you awaken hard with wood
Moist under a single sheet
And excited
Yet, nothing happened or was expressed really
And you are not refreshed only awake
Somewhat depressed

It is a concert night in a hotel along Dinah Shore Drive
In a part of town where every street is nostalgic in name
Dean and Frank rule, and even Gerald Ford gets a mention
Another name performs, a guy you once knew, still tall and
handsome
Talented and plays to 500 or more
You sit at the VIP table alone, until an older women arrives
And you chat her up

Applause, more tunes, some dance
You get to know her a bit
Finale
You head back stage to say hello
Return to this Rachel gal, who looks better as the evening
Gets old, sequins and pearls, long legs, and mostly seems to

have some interest

And you cross the way into the bar, its midnight

The dance goes on
Back and forth stories of woe and inflated bios
Mostly listening now
Married she is, but wants out
Husband dying of some lung disease
She would leave him but he's dying after
All

At her car, I get hugs, some tears, and an old fashioned
French Kiss, who thought anyone did that anymore
Instead of responding, and asking for more, I retreat
Out of fear, fatigue, or maybe, some ethical sense that
That poor dying guy back at the house, just doesn't deserve
cuckoldry
From a one night stand like me
The Motel 6 is cold, the bed hard, the moon glows and casts
shadows, over the lizard that runs over my shoes in the
darkened room
have not had a kiss like that in twenty years or ever walked
away from one
either

CONTENTUS VIVERE PARVO

Some need sofas, recliners, and large puffy chairs
Beds with pillows everywhere
Sheets of satin, wine colored, and mauve
Washers and driers in a closet nearby
Balconies front and back with city views
or
A backyard with a swing, a treehouse
Near the hot tub and lap pool
And a wet bar near the barbeque
Everywhere you turn something big or small
Things of comfort and design that suggest the
Life, well heeled and lived
And enough paper products to blow your nose or wipe your
bottom
Nothing forgotten, out of reach

There are people who live that way
Flush
But I don't need it, none of it
Never have, whether raised that way or innate to my way
Content to live with little
Narrowed down to essentials
A bed, two pillows
A couple canvas chairs that double for the beach

Four plates, a fork or two, a handful of sharp knives
Some cups and glass from bar giveaways
One cable free tv,
And two towels to rotate through the week
One table for everything
Just the essentials, in 500 square feet

Like life easier to manage, keep clean, uncluttered
Nothing to lose of value, except for a few guns and
Those knives my father carried through WWll

When the fire alarm rings at 4am,
set off by a meth head, on the third floor
I can put it all into a bag and get out fast

Vivere parvo
Live with little
Aspire to a grand inner life
An expanded world view from within
And a soul that understands others
And wants to just have nothing
Except your dreams and sanity

MAKERS AND TAKERS

California is not for the meek

Taxes strangle your paycheck

On sales, gasoline, and income too

Freeways crushed by volume

As tons of CO_2 are spewed

Millions dedicated to subways, trains and

Such all supposed to suck us out of our cars

People live on the streets, some off their meds, lost and violent

or both, sucking up hundreds of millions of dollars searching for solutions,

many more working but on the dole

a place where you can get by on someone else's dime

Takers Ayn Rand called them, everywhere

overwhelming the balance of give and get

Marx had the formula, in 1848

"from each according to his ability to each according to his need"

Commies, liberals and later day progressives

All playing the same tune

Raise the makers taxes

Redistribute what they earn

Open up the system so there is always
Money to burn
Expand the government, decide what to do
With what the makers offer up
Release the guys in prison so they can get
Some of this stuff
Pass two thousand bills that imprison every spirit
Challenge every value and declare that everyone of
Every hue and background is really doing well
And not going to hell

A place for takers
Really extraordinary to behold
A massive welfare state
That stops working when the makers do decide
To find the exit ramp
And leave the damn place behind

ON SPIN DRY

No one is awake at 5AM
Unless you have to be
or
whatever is unresolved stomps you awake
like your neighbor on the third floor who
between hip hop riffs, jumps up and down when he
is high, and sings really awful Green Day songs

and not Boulevard of Broken Dreams, I could hack
that once or twice anyway

I try the no mind meditation, open up my chakras,
even Ohm it out
nothing calms me, I am churning from overload of electronic
texts and
the failure to set boundaries with, well, everyone

for solace I turn to the laundry
collect some quarters
bundle up, walk through the buildings
breath in the night bong filled air
and walk for thirty minutes in circles
until the wash cycle is done, put the clothes in the dryer
and watch them spin a bit for my buck and a quarter
entertainment

I run a bit over a hard sand beach

Hear the gulls come awake

Amble over to a locked toilet, too early for the guy with the keys

Crap behind some brush in an alley

Run some more

The sky turns salmon and three dogs run towards me

A fellow older than me, or just more worn out, says good morning

I walk back to the dryer, with a clear head

And an odd feeling of accomplishment

The day ahead can't be that bad.

WORKING FOR LOUIS
NOT KARL MARX

Karl could not know
As he slept on Engels couch
Rent free
What would happen to the proletariat or
Who they would even be in 1968

The struggle for the means of production
The triumph over the bourgeoisie was not that
They would fade, but that we would all become
Them, after the wars, the burgeoning middle class
In Levittown tracts, with actual jobs, and some wealth
In everyone's hands, at least some of it

Until, you are between things
One job going, and the space between the next uncertain
And it does not matter much whether it is about what you
Want to do, you do to earn the rent, and quiet that chill
within you
That you will never work again

It was summer and the teaching job was paused
Bills piled on that kitchen table,
I had moved five times since I left home

Louis Marx had his largest factory nearby in Erie
And I applied to do labor, moving toy parts from enormous
boxes out of trucks to the women on the assembly lines
Forklift drivers piled boxes labeled
Heads and torso
Wheels and axles
and
Male bodies, no arms
And I was the Sherpa who scaled the heights
Took parts into sacks that I carried to the proper
Assembly line
The women were usually cheerful as they joined head and
arms
Put trucks together and hummed to each other
One or two slapped my ass

It was proletarian, Karl would concur
I punched a time card clock in and out
As Louis enjoyed his 25 room mansion in Scarsdale
Where he roamed his 20. 5 acres,
as I found my way to the car
to sleep at lunchtime

The grind wasn't the work
It was Louie and Phil talking about pussy
and sports all through the shift
It never elevated or evolved
Everyday that summer it was about who got laid

And what they did to the poor gals they corralled
Always a few words about the boss, bosses, and the new,blonde
Hire on line #7

Labor Day came and I was spared the Xmas rush
Wondering if Louis and Karl ever met what one would say
To the other
I doubt either would have changed their outlook or philosophy
But Karl might have given up his couch at Engel's house
For a room at Louis' place

THE BURDEN OF MEMORY

The tragedy of time passing
From youth to white hair everywhere
Old age is
What I want to remember I forget
And what I remember is useless and inane

There is the black, Jew, Ethiopian Abdullah
Who was a mystic for men from Rudolph Hess to
Neville Goddard
Who cares that I remember this
My third grade teacher was Miss Ritter who had
Enormous hips and bright red lipstick
Useless
Socrates said before he died
"Crito, we owe a cock to Asciepius. Please. Do not forget
To pay the debt"
Drivel

And forgotten then
The arguments over the bills, the unpaid loans,
Not enough sex or pizza
Hubris' hold for decades on end
Pining for unconditional love, and never finding
Anyone nearby, as easy to be with as the mistress of work

Children raised by others, distance always there, abiding
Separation, even as all those years passed

Men forget the tough, rough and unresolved
Bury it all deeply somewhere, with their tears unwept
Memory distorted, as is all pain, forgotten by design
So you can go on

But a nation cannot forget
Incinerate the regrets, in a bonfire of remorse
Without memory of Wounded Knee, the Edmund Pettus
Bridge
Jim Crow, anti – Semitism, and every other flaw that free
men have
And bring down on others.

Without memory, we chart a crooked path
Turn barbarous, accept tyranny, or worse
Surrender our free will for trinkets of liberty
Political snake oil and disharmony disguised as peace

Must we require our memory to be of failings and triumphs
When they occurred, so we may overcome the sorted past
Accept the pain, unveil our innermost secrets, so
We can act anew with some hope, it all will be recalled
And not damned

LOOSE ENDS

Nitti and Capone had them
Killed
Mailer ended his in over 500 pages
Joe Heller took eight years to resolve
his Catch 22
Jack Ruby tied off Oswald

Unresolved, dangling, matters
Bothersome, somehow
Hanging there before us waiting to be seized
Just or unjust does not matter
the way of things unfinished
a knot required

Rita, Sally, Sabrina
Lunched, and left behind
Awaiting some conclusion they have yet to find

Arguments of daily sort
commitments and promises offered
vainly
to quiet domestic disturbance
keeping it from becoming a bedroom tsunami

the last bar fight

where you were one right hook away
from plastering the loud mouth who cursed
your mother

all loose ends
waiting to be tied
ending the gnawing feeling, they cannot be pushed aside

they all require movement, action, and resolve
and avoided they become more things undone
tossed onto the putrid pile of regret

IN A GLASS CASE IN RED SQUARE

Only the Commies would encase
A dictator exalted for his persistence
to create a totalitarian state that crushed
debate, opposition parties, jailed and murdered
whomever the Cheka could collar
terrorized peasants and intellectuals alike
not unlike the hated Tzars

Romanovs buried in some hole
After being shot and bayoneted
In Yekaterinburg
While Vladimir Ulyanov
rests under glass
As they pass by not knowing

Lenin,his nom du guerre
Born to wealth, flew kites, shot birds, fished
A well regarded lad
Until
His brother Alexander got caught in a plot to kill
The Czar, Alexander III, and was hung for it
Vladimir became Lenin
His friends at 17, left him, the bourgeois deserted him

for all time, he wanted and got retribution
Less Marx, some of that, but more revenge
drove him compulsively

Volatile and driven
Nadya Krupskaya distracted him
With marriage and understanding
Long walks through Alpine paths and
An insatiable passion for his bicycle
And its repair, oiling the chain with the same devotion
That brought him to 17 hour days
Stroke after stroke until his vascular system
Exploded in 1924

All of that was the man
Driven by loss, shunned, shamed by the
Bourgeois, destroyed opposition to gain a hold on
Mother Russia
And still does even under glass

ARE YOU AWAKE?

You can choose your word to describe
A certain mental state when you are awake
And prepared to act around you
The street urchins renamed it 'woke'
To denote eyes open to what it is they pine about
For and constantly, forcing you to wake up to their
Prescribed reality, like it or not, be you or not
Get 'woke' or be drowned by the monster wave of
political correctness

Awake comes from consciousness
That is not externally controlled
It is a biblical feeling of I AM
And once you determine that, the road ahead reveals itself
Before there was anyone else to tell you, there was a
great knowing within you

It is there, to guide you
You own it, it is entirely yours
A gift of creation possessed by all
aware beings where you can determine
How to be and what you want to become

It starts with the declaration I AM
channels through the pathway of what you want

And then when you act that way
Throw away the other views of who you should be
You are then truly 'woke' attuned to you and a destiny
of your making

Throw away the actions and consciousness of who you do
Not want to be
Embrace the actions, look, and posture of what you want
To become
And you will be it

The consciousness is the engine of change
The I AM the spark of creation
Action towards it, always, the key to the door of a new life
Awake to that
You are unassailable, on course and powerful
Once you decide
who you will become
I AM THAT I AM

Sixteen Women 86 Johns

The SS thought they had a way
To encourage inmates to work harder
At their concentration camps
Vile minds believed that the allure of sex
would be a salve for slave labor
at least once in awhile from 8-10 pm most nights
and on Sunday afternoons

Buchenwald had 16 women forced to be
prostitutes, some Jews most not
Stahheber, Zange, Rathman, Fischer, Zimmerman,
Kolbusch to name a few
from records the monster kept
As they watched the men come in, none Jews,
Poles, Slovaks, others who were still able to do the hard labor
15 minutes a session, missionary position only, and
The Kapos had Reichsmark, so they visited more
Every interaction watched and documented
Every thrust observed

On one August night in 1943
The 16 took on 86 inmates
Collected two Reichsmark from each
Had it logged by the guards

And slept until the afternoon of the next day
They were promised they would be released
None were
murdered like the men they serviced
Eventually

At the tribunal after the war
22 Nazi's were sentenced to death
Only nine were executed
All the rest were freed
Only Ilse Koch, the commandants wife remained
To die in prison,
The Witch of Buchenwald

The spirit of the 16 remain
As the wind blows through the room
They gave comfort and humanity
In a word of darkness and doom

THE OLYMPICS OF ILLUSION

Is it all deception
Just a false belief
Some invented impression
A distortion of the senses
That they want us to believe

Politicians and their platforms
Just a game that they always play
To convince their ideas are better
Even though they get more insane each day

Politics has no reality
Only perception of the truth
What they say is,isn't
They think because they expound on it
That will make it so
And they count on the Average Joe being
Stupid or unaware
More likely fed up and angered by the games they play
Back there
Once they asked our viewpoints
Considered our resolve
Thought we had some insights that would help
Create results on things that mattered to us

From pocketbook to Timbuktu
Now totally avoid us, because they know that

We see it as the Olympics of Illusion
this political game they play
Created for just them to parlay

If they could but take action on anything of note
The deficit, trade imbalance, health care costs,
And leave us some cash in the end
Not paycheck to paycheck anymore,
buying Lotto tickets without chances, taxes
Tossed away to pay the debt, and entitlements that are
growing
Everyday Goddam day

They all say its getting better or will if we vote them in
Some facts and honesty would help reverse this trend
That they are all liars after power,
so they can amend
the world the way they see it, and shaft us in the end.

THE THREE WILLS

There is free will, we all have it
Exercise it when we are able, constrained by
others who want us as pawns in their chess game
subverting the choices we might make, if just left alone
but what of those alternatives, do we know what we
might elect, if left to our devices

Old Friedrich Nietzsche thought he knew
As he contemplated in Will Zur Macht
The classic will to power, of course, he did not say
It created some men above us all, perhaps, some would
contend
Mostly nazi's
the bullies of the twentieth century, that there was a master
race
That had the given right and inclination to dominate us all
As likely he pondered a power over our self, as much as
others
To control the best and worst instincts of the species,
Homo sapiens

Between snorts of his cocaine powder, Sigmund could opine
That we were willed to seek out pleasure and that was hard
wired

Into the psyche adrift, caught between Id and Ego,
And we were all so inclined
There was for Freud no higher power or largess we held inside, just basic
Narrow instincts forged when we were young, tortured by our parents, or some
other likely scum

Stuck in some evolution through his stages of growth, going from oral to anal,
Through phallus to gentialia, as the foundation of our desire, always willing for pleasure and away from the pain of all existence

Stuck on his developmental ladder never going up a rung, caring about no one else but our hedonistic, sorry selves

But not all the Germanic thinkers saw us as so crass, there was a will to meaning and purpose that really made us last
Out of Auschwitz, Viktor Frankl, observed his fellow man, trapped in a horror
story nightmare, that few men would escape
Those who controlled their thinking, developed an outlook of grit and grin,
Who never gave their captives the right to obliterate their mind or will
within
The strongest reason for existence Frankl held to truth

Was a person with some purpose, that gave meaning to his every breath
For this he could control and not be taken away, even if that purpose was
Only to survive for another day

Perhaps, we have them all,these three wills of philosopher fame
In varying degrees, some more than others depending on the time in life
When our free will is challenged
and then we must decide whether we are after
Pleasure, power, or purpose

And if a choice is offered, or you are at a great divide
Choose purpose, and seek meaning, and your soul will certainly
Abide.

WOMAN SCORNED

Shakespeare takes the wrap for it
Hell Hath no Fury Like a Woman Scorned
But it is not of his making
It comes from 1697 and another poem not a play
"Heaven has no rage like love to hate turned/
Nor hell a fury like a woman scorned"

The meaning is properly the same
A woman loved can be resentful when the love is all drained
or turns to another, when it is not her call
and the hell of it comes from more rejection than shame

men carry shame when they are tossed out
believing they failed to live up to the shared responsibility
of the coupling, they go deep internally to find the reasons
why, compelled to find an answer from what they have
harbored
deep inside of themselves

oh, yes, they blame the women, there is always much to
quote
often in the most mundane categories, not enough of this,
usually sex, or that
compassion for his plight, a nagging sensibility over finances,
debt and

household blight

For the woman it is even more complex
He was a bad choice, was too internal, distant, and about
himself
He could not expand his horizons, express feelings, or even
listen
Over coffee or a beer, gave more attention to work and balls
and buddies
Than holding her dearly
Ok to drop the bum, on her demand,
but leave her and force rejection
there will always be hell to pay

and if you are in business with such a formidable force
letting her exit, is more than just the same, rejection in this
venue, can bring the hammers of hell on your frame
and crushed you will be by lawyers seeking justice
until you find a sum that will send her off with a victory
and you under her thumb

There may a way to separate
Find another lover
Divorce with equanimity
And not bring scorn upon the woman you once loved
But more likely she will find the rejection a reason to release
the furies of
Hell, and burn you slowly, until you die

DUCK BLIND SUNRISE

Rice and soybean fields overwhelm the landscape
Planted to feed the world, public law 480 in Ike's time
Sent tons from here to fight the Reds
Hard time families now on combines of some size
Rumbling through the harvest season rarely
still

when the farmers rest and sleep
the ducks fly in here across the Grand Prairie
blackened skies over this patch of Arkansas
where "Slick" McCollum set aside a place
where men could come in trucks with shotguns
and settle in the blinds, sit back and talk together
while waiting for the time, when the ducks come from
the fields, like some ancient Hebrew plague, and the
muzzles search for a target, and the triggers pulled unload the
lead

Ducks fall, well trained dogs retrieve
all the practice breaking clays does not ever match
the pure exhilaration of rising from the blind
just West of Stuttgart, between Bayou Meto and Big Ditch
where silhouettes of ducks against the rising sun paint a
scene

a man remembers across his life and times

The most basic of all scenarios reaching back to when
A man could shoot a shotgun and not be damned
or vilified, smile at his companions after he hit his mark
and drive home with dinner, that didn't come out of a
refrigerated box, destined for a frying pan

RED MUSTANG
CONVERTIBLE

I saw it at the World's Fair in Flushing Meadows
In 1964
I was on the Class 122, senior trip
I did not know Iacocca or designer L David Ash
But I saw it gleaming in the Ford pavilion surrounded
By a mob
It was about to be summer, then college, maybe, to some
place unknown
I could not afford a dinner at the Fair, let alone this car
My thoughts were of getting the lawn mower ready for a
summer
making money cutting the neighborhood grass

Seventeen years later in 1981
I saw a 1965, red convertible, 289 V 8
On a pedestal by Third and Beverly in LA
With a moving check in my pocket
About four grand or so, I was magnetized by the notion I
could
Finally own one
I drove it the ocean, top down everyday until the transfer
came
And I was shipped back East

Bought it single, got married
Had kids, the normal ebb and flow
Took it out a few times, just for show
Tried to keep it going, cherry as they say
But life overtook me as it stayed in the garage
It remained a silent symbol of the path of life I
chose

The carefree man who bought it
Gone to the standard life of earning, raising, and climbing
Up and down, hitting rock bottom then getting up seeking
a new
crown.

On one Thanksgiving morning, to a football game
top down in the eastern chill, the engine catches fire
and I am warmed by the orange flames
Have it towed back to the garage, where it sits charred like
my memories

And when the time comes to move back to LA, nine more
years
gone away
I leave the car behind, with the rest of the artifacts of
younger days, no more open roads, only dragons to slay

IT'S ARM DAY

As the years pass
Tossing iron is not new to the muscle fibers
Most of us doing the reps of lore
Again and again
The same sets with weights that once progressed
Memory of your sinews from lifting cast iron plates

Tons of York plates lifted every single week
piles of Ben and Joe Weider magazines and routines
In cardboard boxes under a bed, routines from all the
masters, Reeves, Palumbo, Draper and the rest
that inspired Arnold, Franco and Zane and motivated
Lou

And each day a different challenge to complete the
Chosen routine
Push and pull days for some but most
Do back and legs
Chest and arms
Alternating every other day
To confuse the muscles and force the growth that day

I doubt I have grown larger after the
testosterone retreated, no one else around me
Looks like one single muscle has changed

Still the grunts envelop where the barbells stay
And we all push for biceps to peak on arm day

And when the session is over, every lifter knows who
had an arm day, by the bulge of the inflated bicep
And the popped out brachial vein
from years of pumping iron just to stay in play

BUFFALO WINTER

Winter here lasts
Far past Easter and long before Halloween
Snow falls
On Delaware Avenue to the
centennial place, and covers the grounds
where McKinley took a bullet from that anarchist
that put TR in Charge in 1901

The plow man mounts his machine
And scrapes the roads clean
No matter how much accumulates
You can always make your way

The malls are overflowing
There are no snow days here
A hardy stock of veterans of these long lived
snowfalls

Make their way
Do the errands
Dentist drills whine, pain ensues
Hot plate cooks flip the burgers, pile onions warm in a pile
Parka covered workers clock in each dark morning
And return home in cars and buses salt covered
In the early afternoon blackness

It is warmer by Niagara Falls
Where mist rises and shrouds all nearby
Feels like you are on another planet somewhere past a
nearest star

Spirits do not grow quiet
Business does not halt
Romance still ignites in young hearts
And guys go to their favorite haunts

From this basement apartment
I can barely see, past the 123 inches
That have dropped since October 15th
And encased me, so I close my eyes
And imagine Diamond Head, until
sunrise

WHERE DID CASTANEDA'S
WOMEN GO

He was a liar
A mystic of sorts
A damn good novelist
Who had five witches in his brew
All just vanished
The next day
After he expired from
Liver cancer one April day

Carlos Castaneda wrote of magical
Journeys to Ixtlan, and teaching from a shaman
Named Don Juan
Peyote and mescaline fueled adventures
that gave him fame, even when exposed
it was likely all a dream, or a fraud, or con

He left to raise a coven of women called naguals with
Special powers, like witches most agreed
All gave surrendered to him, a cult in every way

Florinda, Taisha, Amalia, Kylie, and Patricia
All gone the next day
Until they found Patricia's car in Death Valley of

All places, and her bones years later
Suicide perhaps
Other bodies lost in space
Like shape shifter spirits from a Carlos book
Just absorbed by the universe into thin air

What compelled these bright women
Some with PHD's to follow this mystic,
charlatan
Live with him, hear his tales, smoke and trip away
Their lives to a
Destiny unknown
or
Are we all mistaken and it was all true
They are crows and wolves in the Sonoran desert
Who become human at twilight and cook, entwine
And praise their own Gods, in another dimension
While we go nowhere, frozen in our time

KOBE DIED THIS MORNING

When a helicopter exploded
On the way to a daughter's game
In a fog

I know it will not matter
As the years pass away, this January day
Not some milestone for historians
or name to be etched in stone
But perhaps a statue somewhere special
Where fans can pass by and proclaim
That guy was Kobe Bryant the MVP of NBA
fame

He knew at 8 what he wanted
Just to play the game
With an intensity and temperament only
His dedication could ever claim
From a school in Philly he went straight to the LA parquet

Relentless, devoted, improving always
A fire, blazing inside to compete, but more to win
talent touched by something bigger than he was
Driven with desire to always show up
Shoot the foul shot, with a ruptured Achilles
Hit 81 points in a game

End it all with 60 points
No matter how fatigued or drawn
He always brought his game
Relentlessly

The Mamba, he called himself
Always on the attack
out whenever it mattered
Except with his girls, where he was a Renaissance man
Polymath indeed
Who could inspire children while sinking threes
or converse in Italian and Espanol as fluently as he could
play

He put his mind to who he wanted to be
Took his 'knowing' to informing his
Every moment towards a goal to always be improving

Excel at every moment
Even at 3 am, shooting foul shots in an empty arena
Flying back from a bogus court case, so he could play
always be the best, was his pursuit, in all things
No matter what

There was never to be another Kobe
That was always known
That he is gone is

Unbearable to most, tears flow, from the faces of hard men
and women
Who gathered at the place he built in downtown LA
Wearing his 24, carrying candles
Offering their grief for all to see, to a man they loved
Because
He was always game
And he was all heart

CHESS WITH A YOUNG MASTER OF

Accented high school boy
Carried himself mainly through the halls and yard
More serious than the rest at this Cheltenham High School
Some humor but mostly marking time
Waiting for what is to come and next
He always said call me "Ben"
As he moved pawn and rook, aggressively attacked
Always, showed no quarter
Opponents pieces accumulated until the
Denouement

High school boys in 1967 where compelled by
hormones and developing psyche to elemental desires
He had those, but in smaller measure
eyes cast a distant stare towards an ancient place
Where young men carried rifles with foreign names
Kalashnikov and Uzi
patrolled valleys and streets where the patriarchs roamed
and people where shredded in outdoor cafes by bombs
put under tables while eating pizza

His older brother Yani had already gone there
Turning in teenage clothes for the desert camouflage uniform

Already leading other boys and becoming men as the patrols
mounted
Ben played for distraction
Solace and the sense of command it gave him
Over everyone else, a few moves ahead
Always

News comes that there is another attack on his homeland
In 1967, and as fast as a Fool's Mate, two move checkmate
Ben is gone, quietly, nowhere to be seen, with not a single
Good bye

He was there for but an instant
Benjamin Netanyahu, soldier, prime minister to be
off to join brother, Yani, to fight for what they cherished
Whatever, he longed to become, now manifest
Always moves ahead, direct, and focused on only one thing
achievement after a larger purpose,
Preservation

Yani dies at Entebbe
Ben, become Bibi
Then Prime Minister
The chess game continues in the Mideast
There is no Fool's Mate to be played

And no sense anyone will overcome the stalemate

THE GIRL WITH THE PINK TATTOO

Apologies to Stieg and his protagonist
The girl is no agent or super charged heroine phenomenon
Hedy Lamar face, with broad shoulders, and a crushing
handshake
The deep voice and timbre of a Dallas Cowboy cheerleader
Chorus woman legs and sturdy ankles
Where a gaze reveals
A pink tattoo most bizarre, never seen before

What was once the domain of sailors, longshoremen
And crooks, now on grandmothers, accountants, bag
checkers at
Target, and everyone in West LA,
Ink commemorating everything from old school mom and
country
to beers and animals that are not bald eagles
and here this statuesque woman was with
a pink GOP elephant on her right ankle

Putting down the Style section of the NYT, Sunday, in a
casino
coffee shop, I notice she is reading Ayn Rand
not Atlas Shrugged

not The Fountainhead
no more intimidating than that
The Guide to Objectivist Epistemology
Either she is actually reading it or it's the most brilliant
'don't talk to me' signal invented

I know enough Rand, actually have some clue to
Objectivism, mostly about being self centered, fulfilling
Your desires and the world gets better, if we all act this way
Classic Rand crap
So I am not deterred

Start with the book, the message
She warms to it
One afternoon, leads to a dinner
And then a full night, the back and forth bull
Finally to a bed, overlooking the Strip
And on her right butt, in red, white and blue
A petite bald eagle

God Bless America

THERE IS A DREAM WITHIN US

Are we not more than a bio mechanism
of miraculous complexity, who can digest,
move, and contemplate, good and bad thoughts
all at once
billions of cells and firing electrons that renew, recoil and
deliver
with no effort that we can access with no key or code
that we can seek to alter, and destroy
easily, knowing it can harm and not care
gulping booze, chewing red meat, swallowing birthday cake,
candy bars from machines, and every type of potion, pill and
capsule until,it all should stop, from abuse and fatigue
and doesn't

yet, inside that mind there is a sense that
there is more, a dream, we say
once realized or even pursued can offer us
something more, always more than where we are and what
we have
this urge to imagine, construct, Next

is it but a muse, wired by nature or God within us, that
is there so we all don't jump off perches, balconies and every
towns

highest spot?

Why have these dreams
So few of us pursue and those who do
More likely to fail than succeed
What is it of them, for simple things, or life exploding, or
Moving the world, actually, Salk like
More likely of lesser design
A beach house, children, debt free, or what to be
From PHD to dentist to hairdresser
All logical, most achievable, with focus and commitment
It would appear, so dream we do
Endlessly,
a preoccupation with a future
We believe we can control, until the forces
Come, and the dreaming pauses but does not die

What are your dreams, today

WHAT IS FORGOTTEN

How could I know you so well
Through the troubled years when it was all we could do
To find the rent money, pile pocket change on the bed
for gas
And buy clothes at Goodwill

Time passed glacially, all seemed permanent
the Buddhists seemed unaligned with any reality that
nothing is permanent, and all things change
what was in place was stoic and rooted
in a struggle to move on towards something else
we huddled against the frightening reality that it would
always be like this

and your voice soothed, encouraged
its timbre soft, mellifluous, deep enough to drown away
the extraneous noise of everything,
the dissonance of doubt abated

coupled we were so that I could close my eyes and smell
the aroma
at the nape of your neck, the texture of your hair on my face,
the softness of your lower back as my hand settled at the
end of your spine
always enveloped by the warmth of you

how is it now forgotten as fortunes turned
children entered and left
the flame of a life together extinguished
as years burned off like kindling constantly in need of
replenishment
only to be finally a grey /white,ashen pile that has
long before gone cold

Can you long for the other days
When the forces had us locked so closely
Afraid to part, that we could not allow a space between us
So fate might be reversed to have us joined again

Now too much unrecalled
The sound of your voice, the smell of your neck
The warmth
Forgotten is it all
And I cannot retrieve it

BLACKJACK AND BIG PETE

There is a hum, a buzz that electrifies the big rooms in Las
Vegas
The Bellagio has it, but, the Wynn and Encore are bigger
186,000 square feet, MGM Grand 153,000, Mandalay Bay,
160,000
Filled with slots mostly, and tables, some of them for the
only game
Where you have some even chance

Blackjack, with an eight card deck, usually

For my buddy, Big Pete, 6' 4", with John Wayne looks and
a Philly accent
Who count cards, he makes something like 20 bucks an
hour and 100 grand a year
doing only this, for serious work

All the rest is playtime

He is usually at table 45, in Caesars, after 8, with Jimmy the
dealer from Paducah
A single malt at his left hand, and one unlit Camel in his
mouth, that
rolls from left to right sides of his mouth, from hand to hand

Fights off loneliness, to hear him tell it

Wives long ago paid off, his daughters with the grandkids back East

And all his others friends dead.

Cancer mostly of some type, commonly

lung or pancreatic.

No one left to call, text, and his mailbox he checks once a week

Is filled with coupons, nothing else

Never miss him, when I'm there

I'll take one hundred and play, take his nods

And run it up, usually to 500

Never lost, with Pete, twenty years of it

Some damn gathering brings me there

I walk over to his table

Jimmie says he's gone

"where?"

"no gone, sir, gone"

"passed away"

I take out a 100, and play it, like I might win a few

In minutes its lost, all of it

And there is no Pete, with his smokers voice, easy smile

And massive arm to put me in a headlock

The odds he could not beat, got him

Send the Bastard to Jacumba Hot Springs

One small town is shafted, by the big town courts
It has 560 people, a 104 degree hot spring that has a pleasing
sulfur smell, and folks like being rural
and away from the fray of San Diego off old Highway 80

Superior Court judges like it as well as a place
to release the state's most violent sexual predators
the worst of the worst they say
rehabilitated by some hocus pocus man
who declares them threat less, drained of their
violent tendencies, and the judges say
let them be, in a shack paid on the public's cash
outrageous as it may seem
this unique spot is their spot as well
most folks say they should be put in hell

Sexual violent predators they are
One who raped the women, while he put the
Family china on the husband's back so if he moved
The bastard would come out and beat him, when he heard
a crack
Did this plenty of times, destroying lives along the way
Now in a shack with hot tub, all expenses paid

Comfortable he may be with his neighbor James

Who raped two seven year old girls, and a year later a 14
year old

He likes fresh produce, and can be seen buying lettuce and
carrots

With his ankle bracelet for all to see

The folks want them in trailers by the prison

The judges say they are only following the law

The psychologists who say they are ok to go, collect their fees

From the state and feel no remorse

You could not invent this horror tale

of distorted minds obliterating lives

then being set free, and not damned

for all time, forcing a place to comply

when these men, should probably stay away

until they die

there is no angel of death to take them in their sleep

or a masked avenger to blast out their blackened hearts

here instead they stay, not wondering about the next day

but dreaming of what demented act, done or envisioned
again

will get them off, pleasured they are anyway by unearned
freedom

There is no better way to say

How far away we are from justice, and good common sense

Than this waystation in the desert, by a hot spring, where

560 people wonder

Each night, if the demons inside these men will return

And stalk their children and daughters along the dusted paths

WHY IS THE WORLD
THIS WAY

Is there a place somewhere a few million light years away
Where the rules of homo sapiens do not apply
We will all struggle
Some of us will suffer
If you follow the right path, Buddha
Believe in Jesus, Christianity
Tikkun Olam, help repair the world, Judaism
Honor Allah, Muslim
All of that still leaves you to the forces at large

Where

The good drives out the bad
Evil that men do, lives after them
The good interred with their bones, Shakespeare

Our DNA makes it easier to be mean
Than kind
RNA drives us towards conflict, not peace
Rejection dominates over acceptance and
Might can conquer all, evil as it may be
And only rights it, as millions die

Consequences we see are overcome by those

Unintended

Goals are never easily accomplished

All worth having, is worthy of hard work and toil

What comes easily seems not as cherished

Unconditional love always has conditions

From someone for something unexpected

Nothing lasts

All is impermanent

What might be frozen, set, and stable

Will melt, drift and shift away from you

No matter how tight your grip or desire

To hold onto it

In the vastness of all these places, universes known and not

A reverse world must exist that turns it all around

A place where human nature rebounds

And returns to creation, in a celestial Eden found

Where all sins are abated

MORE DIRT THAN GRASS

There was on this practice field
Where teenage boys in helmets and pads
Smashed each other into the ground only to
Prove they could be varsity

Deserve and earn a spot on the high school team
To prove they were men, in the only game they loved to play
That could give them glory for a few years, and help pass
The next years away

It was a linear way to be someone of consequence, walk
the halls with the swagger that only football could bring
Scholarly pursuits, would never bring what every young man
Wishes, a rep to take from study hall to the back seat of
your dad's
car on a Saturday night, at a make out place called Little
City, or
parked behind your uncle's bakery, where you could smell
her perfume
and the fresh bread baking at the same time

there was always blood in the dirt, and on your jersey
big shouldered guards and tackles who seemed 21 and
bearded
knocked you over

repeatedly,
until your nose would bleed from both nostrils
and the coach would pull you side, and let you know
you made the team

the blood, the refusal to stay down, and the occasional sack
on that ego fueled QB got you there

everything you became
emerged from that practice
field of dirt and little grass
where what seemed a fight for reputation, and ass
was instead the crucible for the nosebleeds of life
the knockdowns of the journey
and the will to get up
again and again

THE FIELD OF SORROW

There is a field of sorrow
Where nothing ever grows
Miles and miles of scrub grass and sand
No sounds come at dawn, nothing crawls around
A sky always grey, promising no greater light
No sun rises or sets

No one wants to be here long
Just get through it as they can
Hoping to maneuver quickly over the cold terrain
On their way to another place where it might
even rain

everyone comes here sometime
where they certainly do not want to go
an unplanned destination where your
darkest feelings grow to consume your
thinking awake and when in repose

there are those who spend a lifetime here
aimless hikers all, who have lost their direction
and scream for night to fall, unable to exit, stuck in
a morass of feeling lost with no rebound
others so frightened by the place, they do not rest or fall
but walk until exhausted towards some other goals, and

fight the miles of sorrow, with a simple hope that they will
come to its end, and move on

Across the field of sorrow, the horizon is not gone
There is an end to it, if you do persist
Afraid of it, and fearful it may take you down,
All your dreams destroyed as you wander in circles
And finally waste away
It can end you there and then and
thinking of it will make it so

EVERYBODY HAS A DREAM

Suppose that you could have finally that
Dream you have held within you
Is it still there to be revealed or is it buried so deeply
That it must be mined from within your soul
And having hit the vein of it, would it still emerge?

Would it be a dream of youth that seemed so bold
Immediate and urgent
Usually small and basic then to
Have a real friend,
a father who talks to you and smiles once
in a while
for the taunting bullies to just leave you alone
that someone will sit next to you at recess and not steal your
Twinkies,
that she is a girl with a soft voice and is funny
Being smart in class is ok, finally

Or

Having enough money to buy
A season ticket for anything, the Corvette,
A sharkskin suit, a week in Maui, a large screen television,
A recliner that vibrates, a shotgun, four years in college to
become

Lawyer, doctor, chemist, PHD in something,
Engagement ring, down payment on the first house, pay off
Mom's mortgage,
Bury Uncle Joe, pay for the kids college, handle the hospital
bills,
Retire away to some warm spot, where you can dream about
what you
Dreamed about

Or

Are the big dreams still there and viable
That just might change the world
Find a cure, create a noble scheme, offer up a novel, or
something
on a screen
touch someone with your kindness, save a person damned,
show the path to
anyone lost along the way

If one night you awaken and a dream is realized would it
be just
What you held inside
or has that hope been rotted like fruit left by its tree
something that once ripe now shriveled of no use or just not
meant to be

there is no hand to touch us,

no power that will come in the darkness
whatever our dreams may be,
we must find them, and decide when we can
whether they still have power over us,
and drive us forward again, or should they
be abandoned and
new ones
imagined now

I WISH I WAS XENOPHON

Everyone wants to be a polymath,
a man of many things, accomplished in all of them,
effortlessly when observed, transcendent in ability,
possessed of grit, sensitivity, and free of all vice and sin
hard to find one man who is in this modern age, everyone
doing
everything in a mediocre way

Not for Xenophon
The commander of the Greeks 400 years B.C.
took the Ten Thousand from Persia to Armenia
winning more than he lost, developed the strategy of
flanking, and some
new attacks, even codified how to retreat in battle and not
be decimated
lesser know that Alexander, at 30 he was in his prime
conquered with his mercenaries, then Sparta, unscathed
was he
all this time

Known for more than his warrior spirit he was philosopher
and writer both
Even wrote of how Socrates influenced his youth. Telling
tales of fighting off vice

and choosing virtue by all who cross his path
And he writes of self control and striving to be better and helping others be the
same.
Defends Socrates refusal to fight his captors, and die at his own hand

Xenophon ate with his common soldiers, slept on the same poor beds, always kept their welfare in mind, and always kept them fed
Wrote volume after volume on topics from virtue to battles, and the defense of intellect
And action to preserve a place where men could contemplate serve themselves and their Gods
To him a good general was awash in conflicts
Gentle and brutal
Capable of caution and surprise
Lavish and rapacious
Generous and mean
Able to attack and know when to retreat

There are busts and statues of him that show a sturdy look
A warriors' body and thick ankles and wrists
But a smirk as well revealing an inner man
Who put his mind to great ideas, as critical to him as any military stand

I am not Xenophobic, perhaps, but being like Xenophon is
not so bad

A man from Greece, who knew more than how to use a
sword and lance

who put words into volumes that establish his place in the
history

of man ......If I get to be 77, what will the poets think
of me....

LET'S DO LUNCH OR A ROOT CANAL

Dating should not be this difficult in the digital age
There are apps for all the ages, kinds, and hues
Electronic places where the religious can converse
And swiping left or right gets you in front of someone
to
Profiles of these women who reveal what they want to
Bring, truth or not, just to attract you
All these gals after the same man or so it seems to me
Gentle, funny, a gourmand, handsome somewhat, good
listener,
Likes animals, kids, and has a PHD

Better to throw away the apps and go the old school way
Meet a person, who knows a person, a cousin or an aunt
A referral that they might actually want to meet you and
Have a face to face
Just lunch, they always say, no big ask or damage to be done
to anyone

Meet with a few aunts, and cousin and a mother of so and so
All handsome, well appointed, intelligent with no doubt
but, all tied so firmly to their narratives that it makes the
luncheon

Last, and last, go on and on
Being a grand listener, I nod and support the dissertation
on family, exes, interests, hopes, some dreams, bucket lists
and all
of which I am not included in any of it
Staying away from me, except in some perfunctory way
Until the waitress comes, and a sigh comes my way

It should not be so painful, as arduous, attempting to find
some
common place or ground
but the dentist and the root canals were somehow more
sublime
Pain at first and then removed, here the reverse is so
So difficult it is to avoid the anguish of two souls longing for

A connection that may stop the pain inside
That comes from being alone
Attempting to bridge a great divide
With a lunch at a busy downtown hotel
And it costs less than the visit to Doctor Demento

PUNXSUTAWNEY PHIL

Nothing more than a woodchuck
Marmota Monax to be precise
Lives ten years on average and is usually left alone
Except on the second day of February
When old men, with thick waists, covered by long coats
And heads in top hats gather in Punxsutawney
to pull one named Phil from his hole of comfort
for some damn ritual, as pure silly as could be

47 per cent accurate the predictions of winter coming
or spring, a party ensues like the Druids had when they
signaled
the coming and going of the season of spring
15 Phil's most likely, who lived a woodchuck's life, except
When they were on television, flying to a talk show with a
hyperactive host, being grabbed by the gut and held high
for the obligatory toasts, so desperate they are at Gobbler's
Knob for spring to arrive

And it would all go on, until they all tire, yet there
Is still an allure to this ritual Groundhog Day, a regularity
to it
That makes it seem ok, to roust a critter from his lair and
replay

It every year

But, now you cannot shoot, touch or fondle an animal without

groups to say do not

They want Phil replaced with an intelligent robot

Let the woodchucks retire and create a machine that will

Predict the weather in some scientific way

Who can say that's not valid, with a politically correct sashay

Better results, and no one gets bitten on future

Groundhog Days

THROUGH A POET'S EYES

It is noisy all the time, not the trolley or the trucks
Mother's screaming for their kids to come to dinner from
the stoop
in Washington Heights or Sheepshead Bay
not the deli guy bellowing for who has number 12
or the cop breaking up a family fight
"nothing to see here, nothing to see here, move on!"

Old noise is quiet these days, the cacophony that was
The backdrop of every single day, subsided into phones and
Devices, no one speaking, except in texts, the tonality of
communication
forever altered. Who knows what you mean, with the damn
context

everyone is a pundit, critique and savant
millions of electrons consumed and blown into space
inconsequential, but taking up time, energies and space
unending dialogue of nothingness, not advancing the
human race

what is actual or fiction gets harder to ascertain
fakes, and bias overwhelm your limited brain
essential truths are victimized, murdered by partisans
everyone with an agenda that only serves their cause which
is to subjugate us all, machine wash our minds, and deposit us

cleansed on a beach where the ocean is gone

the only defense is to see the world as a poet
detached and apart
reflecting upon the deceit, fraud, malfeasance on our psyches
the hijacking of our evolution to throw us back in time
stripped of all sense of balance, empathy and any depth of
knowledge
outside of our own narrowly focused truths

Once eternal truths obliterated by sending one mean Tweet
Fighting only virally, never offering a name
Anonymous assassins of character and always laying blame

See the world as a poet
Neruda in a cottage atop Isla Negra
Fondling Matlide Urrutia that mistress of all time
Where the dawn awakens, but does not disrupt
observations, synapses of creativity, etching out a purpose
from room where the old noises fade as you write
hoping that the act itself will suddenly put it all in order
inhale, and exhale a thought that silences the chatter
for a moment of contemplation
The poet is saved by his craft
No matter how poorly written well done
Unheralded and forgotten
It is the Poet's view, The Poet's life that my save us
All
As the years go by

CIGARETTES, SEX AND A CAR

Not more than eleven in a school yard
Named after an Admiral, Spruance who won us the battle
of Midway
In an alcove, huddled with four others and
That older guy named Ray
Who had a pack of Camels and gave each a one
They all lit up and started smoking
As I did as well
Knowing inside myself that my Father would beat me
Into hell

Tobacco smoke came in and out of their
Nostrils and their mouths but I could not manage to
Keep the cigarette in my mouth
For my first time, brought a burning and bad taste
And inhaling I could not do
Gave it up there, and never practiced to become
A smoker with all the others, and I stood alone through
All those teenage years, unhooked by any of it
And saving my young lungs

There was talk among us all,mostly lies and tales
of who had sex by whom and the odd places where it
all occurred in car back seats, in basements and garages,

164

a rec room at uncle Joe's, or a living room couch, beds seemed
out of the realm of all our boyhood dreams.

There was talk
of baseball bases from first to third to home,
it seemed there was a lot of in and out discussion but I doubted
anyone really ever got laid
the guys who actually completed this adolescent rite
where more than likely circumspect about it and fought to keep it
to themselves, unless they were just louts, and damaged reputations of
the girls who did put out

Better for me it was than that first cigarette
Some pleasure in it, mostly of conquest
Certainly glad it was over, in something of a flash
And could pursue the sex less pre-occupied as the senior year
Eclipsed,
becoming more adept at it as the tension subsided
Over if it would ever come to pass,
And it did bring some swagger to my walk that was not there before

None of it defined me, these firsts of those years

They where not seminal to my sense of self or what I might achieve

Independence and free will issued by the state

With a license in my wallet and my father's Pontiac

I had responsibility and purpose to get from here to there

No one on my case as I turned the corners, to the straightaways

along the Roosevelt Boulevard, imagining nothing more grandiose

than the dreams of regular folks

Three firsts that may define, how a boy will see the

world when he becomes mature, if that ever actually

transpires that we go from boy to man, or is it all so indelible in

our cells and memory that it holds us there, frozen in time

Never smoked, anything in all these years

Had some sex, as rarely now as in that boyhood time

And when I roll the window down and the wind gets in my

Hair, the troubles can still fade, but rarely do.

OUTCOMES

Aristotle wrote of the Golden Mean

Sartre of men adrift overcome by ennui

Nietzsche had his ubermensch

Socrates championed happiness and reason that did sway

The 280 of 220 who voted that he die

Kant offered up imperatives of the categorical kind

Locke claimed a social contract between us and the
governments we create

Ayn Rand put her claims of selfishness into massive novels

To struggle through

All offering insights to what makes the world the way it is
epistemology

deep thoughts without prescription of actually how to live

let alone what you must do to get the results you want

nothing in their volumes, tomes and teachings of how to

close the gap between what you want and how to get it
achieved

Outcomes are what we are after, practical philosophy

street advice, where we think we will just get there by

trial and error of some degree

but there is another way to chart the path you
want

reverse engineer the outcome from result to inductive sum

Will the result come to you by acting on your own
If what steps must you take to go it all alone
Or do you need allies, who are they and what will make they
Come by your side to join with you in this outcome quest

What is the celerity of the need is it urgent
Can it be delayed?
Timing is,if not, everything certainly plays a role
And have you thought through the consequences as you
move
Along the way
Will unintended ones ever come into play

Outcomes are real
Move you ahead or hold you back
Street philosophy more likely to get it done than what
The philosophers have to say
Or ever will, if there any anymore

SHIRTLESS IN FEBRUARY

Warm enough to run along the bay
Turn towards the Pacific
Volleyball players stripped down, their girlfriends digging
In their thongs

Clusters of friends in canvas chairs
Having illicit beer drinking games
Two old women dancing to Despacito a hit
of Reggaeton
a smile across every face that
sends a luminescent vibe into the cloudless sky

All their worries absorbed in sand and sea
Whoever died, crashed, overdosed, divorced
forgotten for just one day

Whatever it is they do in other places from Manhattan to
D.C. bundled against the wind and the ills they hold within
Bring them here and take off your shirts, skirts and pants
Turn your face towards the sun, and let your worries go away

COURAGE MAKES ME CRY

As a boy the eyes are mostly dry
Only scrapes and humiliation ever brings a tear
Shame mostly turns a face away and tears come
Reluctantly to be hidden from mom and dad
No crying on the fields of play or because you are
alone

Old school men rarely shed a tear
no matter they may portend, even when surprised by some
sad song or unexpected movie scene
stoic when hit in the face, mad enough to scream
no tears will come, from a nightmare or a dream

when a boy stands up to the schoolyard bully
knowing a beating is still his lot
defends a skinny friend taunted by the mob
won't let his sister be mistreated by the jerks who
want to get into her pants
will not step back when he is right
courage in too short supply

These acts bring tears to my eyes

everyone in the boardroom panders to the CEO
except for one well dressed guy, risking everything

just to be honest that day
that politician on Capital Hill who votes against the caucus
even though his
career ends with just one vote
the women who finally leaves the bastard after years of being
betrayed

Their courage makes me cry for all of those who never, ever
back away

Courage comes from common folk
Against all those in charge, the mighty without conscious
No sense of what is fair, right, honest
Left to the rest of us, to say no, that cannot be or stand
Something here is wrong to be turned right no matter
what the
Cost, busted nose, bloody face, lost job, and all the rest
The greatest risk is to do nothing at all suffer cowardice

This display of courage makes me cry,
and
I pray for more tears

MAGENTA WALLS AND MIRRORS FOR A CEILING

Trains are halted, pulled into their stations
Conductors home with families, no lunch pails to pack
Union jacks picketing
The rattle of subway and train silenced
An army of commuters march across the Brooklyn Bridge
Others hitch a ride, some into motor pools crammed with
Neighbors for the ride, a few stay home, until it becomes clear
That this transit strike is intransient, it will take some time
To get them to a table for some sort of compromise

Crafty long term Mayor Koch, popular with many
Stands at the bridge, and encourages the throng
With a signature refrain
"How am I doing ?"
Amended as an alternative
"How you doing, how you doing"
As they stumble past in the April morning haze

A few of us petitioned our bosses to let us stay
In the city for the duration and leave our families in the burbs

No hotel rooms left to populate,so they found us rooms
From other executives who cashed in their accrued days
And flew away to Bimini or Cancun

I spent the next few weeks in high rise by the park
With walls colored in deep magenta carpet, that I thought
Would be on the floor, and the ceiling was a mirror that made it
Hard to sleep at all

This pied –a-' terre designed for amour and more than just shacking up
Underneath the television, there was a box of erotic tapes, that old men
kept hidden in those days, before the internet, a pornocopia for trysts

I wondered who he might be, a sturdy, master of the universe, in starched shirt
and 4,000 buck Brunello Cucinelli suit

Refrigerator with fruit, cheese, and bread
More than enough to take you to the end of the episode
And when I ran the park after dark, the rats seemed unperturbed
By all the footsteps getting in the way of their worn tracks
And it all seemed absurd

CROSSING THE MOJAVE

Used to drive from the Cajon Pass to Caesar's
Over 85 all the way
Back in the day when there were car alarms to spot the
troopers
They mostly chased the guys in red Corvettes and muscle
cars
And left guys in sedans mostly alone
It was always dark, after work, and the desert on either side
was black, the big dipper was planetarium bright, and the
road was
straight

Troopers begat helicopters that begat radar and you were
always
Under big brother's gaze, so I slowed down under 80, but
found I luxuriated
In that ride, ambling by

The biggest thermometer at Baker
An old resort, Zzyzx, was the last word in health before the
big war, now a research center of something
where I came across
Two girls in a convertible, taking snapshots of themselves
bare

breasted, who said, "Hi, Mister", like they did this everyday

Peggy's Sue's diner with a 50's motif where a stack of hot cakes is barely

under six bucks, and you look out at a cordon of metal dinosaurs against the desert sky, when its 102 in August

artists seem to prefer dropping their public art off the highway and from time to time I've seen old tanks, colorful obelisks, an array of crosses to the dead, and

some

just to connect us sinners to the Lord

no matter how fast you travel you will see the ten commandments,all of them

like a Burma Shave ad of old, and the symbols of three faiths at the end of it

never saw anyone stop to pray,

I'm one of the few who just a mile

away from the Nevada line, turned off into a town with a general store,

trailers, a four room hotel from the gold rush time, and the claim it

is the "gateway to the Mojave"

a fellow for the guy who owned Nipton, wanted to sell it to me, after I had

a root beer and shot a few rounds of the my .38 into some jugs by the solar panel

array that powered the place

he sold it before the old man died to a Japanese outfit that wanted to

grow week, and ship it to LA

then there is an intense luminesce
tall, mirrored towers bring from this place
Ivanpah a solar power megalith
knocks out 392 megawatts, from 175,000 heliostats
Cost you and me 1.6 billion in loans, takes care of a small city
But stores nothing, and gets started every morning with good ole'
Reliable natural gas

Missed all of it, at 85 mph
Taking it in now
Less compelled to play, chase the fortune, that has eluded me
And inhale the dry air, turn a face to the sun, and convince myself
It is just good enough to be on this desert road.

10,000 Hours to get it Right

The cowboy in Utah used to say it
Will take 10,000 hours to get anything new right
The 3 R's of cowboy
riding, roping, and rodeo
by right he opined, just get 'in by, not being good at it
that adds up to almost three years, everyday, awake and
engaged

Persistence is required, being hardy to your core
Rising to do it, learn it, because it is your desire
to excel and overcome the pain, boredom, and distress
of what it takes to get there none the less

Cowboy claims it works for learning French, or ballet
Selling Cadillacs or even Ford trucks on display
Welding and carpentry too
And maybe how to woo, Mary Lou
Unlikely, even if he says so

The problem is not how many hours you put it
But is it worth it to you, when the years are done
What have you parlayed, or betrayed
to master
The task, did it more than provide, did it mean anything
Valued, perhaps, beyond the almighty buck

Did you spend the 10,000 on just one thing
Put a string together of 10,000 more
Offer any of those hours so you could adore
Not ignore, what you brought into this world

Cowboy knows as the hours blew by
That the 10,000 hours were but a way to pass the time
From the clock that ticks towards that final chime

NUMBER 8 TRAIN TO COVINGTON, LOUISIANA

June is hot, usually, in Louisiana
Was in 1892, in New Orleans
When Homer Plessy put himself
on a train to Covington

not much to fret over if he was white
which he was not, and sat in the white-
only car
he planned to be in trouble wanted to state for
all that separate cars were wrong
The conductor was in on the scheme
And told him to move on down
And when he refused,he was
Attacked, handcuffed, and jailed

The set up was to decry in court that
Separate but equal was a sham
Violated that new 14th amendment
Not so said judge Ferguson righteous bigot
he was,
that "Separate Car Act" is a damn good
law he declared without even impaneling a jury

This made its way to the Supreme Court, you know
Plessy hoped they would say it wasn't so, that separate but equal just
had to go

7-1 said absolutely, NO!

Famously, Justice Harlan claimed, "Our constitution is colorblind"

Which is was not until 1954, when Brown v Board of Education shut the door
on a doctrine of Jim Crow that 54 years before had to go, but was allowed
and required more Homer Plessy's to be brave, in the face of a perniciously
discriminatory age

Plessy made shoes, did hard time in warehouses, handled life insurance for others,
Paid his 25 dollars fine for boarding the wrong train, passed at 61
One shoemaker, on a humid, uncomfortable day, who got to say this is
wrong, and must be changed, and thought enough of American justice that
there was a remedy afoot, that took five decades to act
But it did

THE GAPS

There is a space between who we are and
Who we want to be
An expanse between what we do and what
We know we should do
A chasm that separates us from our authentic essence
And how we appear to the world

Gaps that define our day to day choices from
The ones that elevate and evolve or hold us
In a homeostasis, stuck on one side of the precipice
Unable to leap across to our better selves or build a
Bridge to our actual, awaiting, if unknown
Destiny

Small indiscretions
An enticing doughnut, an abundance of protein
Cow carcass, steers, fowl enough to fuel
A full platoon
Anything fried, stuffed, glazed, pureed

Indulgences of emotions released in anger, disgust
Humiliation, lost across a lifetime of missteps
Thoughts becoming phrases out of joint, hurtful, demonizing
Dumb and misguided
Yet, uttered in that gap

Between thoughtful consideration and prideful boasts
or avoidance of some humiliation, so genomic to be
unavoidable

the gaps are always there
a knowing speaks and rumbles within
too easily avoided and dismissed
that allows us to believe that we can act today in a certain way
even though it is clear, it is a rutted path far, far away
from reaching up and pressing on
to do what we should to improve, be better, healthier,
smarter, kinder, empathic, a good person, in our eyes and
anyone else, who cares enough to be watching

when they are all closed
there is nirvana, self- actualization, satori
the sages say,
but what do they know?

THE MURDER OF RUGGED INDIVIDUALISM

T.R. had everything,but his health, with determination and grit forced
everyone, even a nation to be energetic and full of his optimism

Jack London did whatever he wanted, mined gold, sailed to Hawaii in a boat he
built, surfed, ran for office, wrote and drank non stop, boxed with his wife, and
lived a life on fire

Kirk Douglas, gobbled by life, devoted to what he envisioned, and became
iconic, in 90 films,
broke the back of the McCarthy blacklists, courageous as Spartacus, and just as
hard ass, to save Dalton Trumbo from oblivion

Burt Lancaster, circus acrobat, to roles on screen of depth, pathos, and anti-
heroes, he was Gantry, Earp, and even a beaten old man on the Atlantic City
Boardwalk, or Archibald, "Moonlight" Graham

Andrew Carnegie, got to the U.S. at 12, parlayed his investments into millions,

Built a steel company,

sold it to Morgan for 300,000,000,

then gave it all away

To everything that has his name on it today.

His positivism, dictum was in three pieces

Get an education; make all the cash you can; give it all away

before you die

Henry Ford, was destined for the farm, until his mother died

he became a machinist, who had a vision of a mass,consumer economy, that he

forged with

The Model T, inventor he was not,

but the market man, less philanthropic, a dedicated man of pure hate and

prejudice, saw the world only his way

General George Patton Jr., always led from the front, was a tactical genius in

battle,

had no tact otherwise

most resourceful, clever, bright soldier who could quote Clausewitz and curse to

high heaven

Duke Wayne, seemed to own the zeitgeist of strong men
with complex inner mechanisms, often not expressed
Ethan in the Searchers, Sgt. Stryker as a Marine on Iowa
Jima,
Most rugged, Rooster Cogburn, or everyman
there was a man driven to have his own way, but with an
inner awareness,
that it would not always be that way

Rugged men all

Most all from impoverished starts, distant fathers, hard
working stiffs
Some drunks, some worked to death, others just gone
Mothers more revered and deeply loved
By their own effort, and choice, not
Without good fortune, hard work, a break or so
And the time they lived in where such values were actually
Embraced
Working hard, being willful, and enduring against all odds
Applauded not demeaned
A straight forward age, Golden it has been deemed
Not serene or filtered, lived honest and open, not overly
complex
murdered by a wind of change that made all of that suspect
requiring a quieter presence, no man portrayed that way
A betrayal of a self that was once rugged and pure
Productive and embraced

Now so cut down to be almost entirely erased

Find a Kirk, or T.R, Carnegie or Ford today

Where might they be in hiding

Men of backbone, simple values, and a belief that

The rugged man in a free society can invent, produce,

sustain or win at anything, against any odds, anywhere

A Playground for All Seasons

There is no one here on this battered field where I played
Football, tackle and touch, ran routes until I was sore, ripped
off skin of elbow, knee, and ass

Convinced the Green twins, Lenny and Bo, both guards, on
varsity, one summer
That I could make the team, and did, by slipping through
them full of sweat and
slim enough to slide between, until tackled by another
unshaven stiff named Dyak
who taught me humility

The basketball rims faded orange with chains, mostly
unhooked dangling
Now in reach, if I could but get off the ground, as I did
when the rims where
white and a new cotton net was beneath them
Everyone had a hook, a jumper, but
there was no three shot, or a dunk, even if anyone could, it
just did not exist, even
on Wilt's court in West Philly, not yet

I would play until the girls came by to watch, play a bit
more, and then glide with
them back to a basement rec room nearby, for the give and
take of what passed
for mating

Today,three boys are hitting fungo
And they let me take the long, light bat, and swat out a few
grounders
Then I wave them back and nail a few fly balls, muscle
memory returns
For a few swings, and they laugh at "Pops"
Sitting on a decaying wooden bench, still green painted,
The sounds of the diamond come back, the sun warms a face
Now wrinkled, once smooth and tan from an entire summer
here

Is there anything I did not learn here
In this playground of humility, risk, desire,
Loss and gain?

Any emotion I did not have
Pain not experienced, exhilaration missed?
No dreams launched, perhaps, no grand scheme
Only the moments hooked, by the seasons of sport
And comradeship, now faded

It never seemed it would end

The thought did not come to mind

Each movement was for itself, every throw, run, pitch and

Bruise accepted, not rejected

What field am I on now

This field of modern, adult life

That is grind over joy, hoping to move on

But not

EXISTENTIAL THREATS

Overused by anyone wanting to support their contention
That your values or beliefs are threatened
A point of view so dearly desired and expressed
A way of life in totality, about to be obliterated
By an evil force, only defeated by massive, collective action
In one direction

Man made mostly bubbling up out of a volcanic will
To power, domination, aggrandizement
Nazi's, Commies, Asian emperors, in the 20th century
Radical Islamic fundamentalists now
Destroyers of free will for the same thing
Control of everyone and everything
Subjugated to one world view

Crushed by free people with force of arms

Not all threats as easily blown from the stage of existence
Malthus thought too many of us, would outstrip resources
Welcomed famine, disease, and the above wars to thin
out the
Great Unwashed
But population less the fright than what
The throngs did as the population grew
Fouling water and air, boring holes in ozone

Scalding and scraping the crust
Texas size islands of plastic floating atop
Polluted seas

The grandest ET is hardly biblical imposed by no
monarch or dictator
Good old gluttony, excess, putting anything
From hand to mouth
Exploding guts and waistlines, damaging blood vessels
Organs hard to place thyroid to pancreas
Cancer havens of life styles gone beserk
That morning bear claw is more likely to wipe you out
Than the power plant in the Arizona desert

The mouthy have's, the later day socialists
Proclaim climate change is the ET of now
As they eat away at their rib eye, polish their boots,
And fly off to Cabo
Who knows where we are in this advance and retreat of ice
sheets?

Just as likely celestially, Jupiter moves erratically or spews
some
inner crap and it arcs our way, from some asteroid belt, and
That existential threat is a flash that ends it all for us, blows
a crater
in the Yucatan, again
, and we dissolve with our cellphones, apps, Tesla's

and endless texts into unrecognizable ash heaps
becoming the second oldest species to live and die here, T
Rex and his buddies
outliving us by many 100 millions of years

And while we are awaiting that
The whining #novacforme
Cordons of pale faced, and stupid parents will eventually
Allow an otherwise controllable virus or disease to
Strike with Malthusian accuracy, putting Measles, Mumps
And Rubella back in our lives

Pick your existential threat
Strike out against it, if you must
Knowing that what the mouthy purveyors
Say it is, probably isn't

ALL IS NOT WELL IN CHANAKYAPURI

It is here where the US Embassy in India rests
A safe district in New Delphi, barbed wire and Marines
Keep it secure
Not for a 5 year old, of a staffer
When parents went away
a housekeeper of 25
Raped her

The Mahatma would cry
For all the women defiled
In New Delhi, the one attacked by a dozen men with
An iron rod, penetrated many times
On a bus, then tossed on the road
Dead she is, family hoping for mercy and redemption

The 11 year old who came for
Soda laced she did not know with
drugs, so she could be raped over and over
and filmed to amuse, while they cut her
with their knives

Then in Hyderabad
Four jackals took a teen and

Raped her, until she was unconscious
Cops found them and shot them dead
Even though they were unarmed

The assaults go on
In a democratic place so vast
heinous crimes can be lost, absorbed by the struggle
not of independence but pure existence
and the good men scream, and mothers cry for
justice, in a place where there is damn little of it
for a five year old, waiting for her mother to come
home to that Embassy in
the Chanakyapuri district in New Delphi

ICE ON THE WINDSHIELD

It is there every morning
This thin layer of it, some mornings thicker
Reflecting back the orange hue of the rising sun
Initial challenge of the day requiring
Brute force or not
Requiring a decision before coffee or
conversation

Memory of a line of cars on my row house
street, where the warriors of Iwo Jima, Saipan,
the Ardennes, and Midway
started the cars, with grey exhausts creating a low
cloud below the tree tops, as they sat at the
kitchen tables with their wives, turned to the sports
page and returned to a warm place, hit the wipers and went
off to a place that gave them a piece of the American Dream

Never saw my father scrape a windshield

So why was I reaching for a lame scraper in Peoria
a large red one in Erie, from a supermarket chain
that pocket sized one, emblazoned Go Blue, in Ann Arbor
a hockey stick contraption from the Buffalo hockey squad
a piece of cardboard in West LA, where the ice regime should
never come

broke most of those devices in rage, disgust or both

some mornings clarity would come
and the engine would run
listening to a traffic report and morning talk radio jabber
a morning ashram inside, bundled against the wind chill
waiting to be warm, and the melt coming
of that ice shield

all those years of it
scraping, breaking plastic in anger or petty despair
vowing to never face it again
fleeing the tyranny of the ice, not wanting this
repugnant morning metaphor any longer

still aware that
if it was not the ice it would be something else

FROM STONE TO SAND

Transformation, becoming something else
At least churning what we have or are into
Another version of us, a process embedded in
evolution
no cellular entity stopped, glacial though it may seem
in a Redwood forest, a perfect pearl slowly growing, in an
oyster somewhere
adolescent spurts to maturity, hitting three pointers on the
parquet

cells changing, mystic, massive, morphing
from what is to what evolves, unceremoniously
an untouched design requiring nothing more than existence
doing what it must do, with no tick tock, of any other
purpose
than to unavoidably be and become
until the cosmic stop sign appears

life forms digesting,all around them, whatever they need
to be
Lithoredo abatanica, a tube shaped mollusk
That burrows into river beds, of shipworm species
Usually eating wood, not in this Philippine river
It eats stone, turns it into sand

Not a scientist can tell why
Other than it does to survive
Inexorable is their reply

As it is for us bombarded by thoughts, opinions
Demands, commands, and directions after our
Essential selves, seeking to penetrate to our cellular essence
Morphing our trajectory, once naturally set, now transformed
by ecosystems so resolute and forceful to alter our genetic
plan
perhaps we were meant to turn stone to sand, or evil to good,
wood into lumber, be an eternal light of optimism

nothing forces that shipworm from its path
the redwood from excreting its rings for hundreds of years
or the transformation of an irritating grain of sand from
becoming that perfect pearl
what would we become if just left alone?

AFRAID OF

What are we afraid of
Failure, embarrassment, death,
Poverty, disease, our mother's dismay
Father's wrath
Burning alive in a stalled car
A road rage bullet, loneliness, if we live long enough
Go figure it out, what you are afraid of

Write it out, say it, realize it is all useless
This fear, holding you back from greatness,
Wealth, or even, God forbid, happiness
Are you even afraid of that?

Joy unknown, regarded less than struggle,
Less than hard work, long hours, all this
Puritan bullshit, Spartan values leading to
Life plans dashed, discarded, degraded

All out of fear of

Rejection, so what now, putting more off
Shoving everything down deep
Afraid to force what could be, for what is settling for
Accommodating, just calling it a life
Rutted, existence of patterns familiar

But comfortable more shackled, with chains
Still wrapped around neck and balls, as real
As those for slaves, but by your own hand
Forged, bound to a post doglike

Shitting in the same hole awaiting
The identical bowl of dead meat, licking from the
Same saucer
Pretending you are free, held back by what you are afraid of

In a carotid artery, sleepers hold
Not on your neck but on your soul
Easily released with but one, courageous act
of just letting go
The only fear that ever mattered
Or needed to be overcome

Up There by Lincoln's Nose

Borglum hired 400 men and a few women
to blast and carve away in the Black Hills
the faces of four presidents, that most folks could not
name today for a gift certificate to Wal Mart

the youngest was Nick Clifford at 17, who for 55 cents an
hour hauled men up a winch 5700 feet, to work on Lincoln's
nose, he roamed up there himself
planting dynamite for Gutzon

wasn't his stone skills that got him hired
he played a damn good game of baseball
so Lincoln Borglum hired him, to field a team to
beat the others in and around that South Dakota
place, where they were cutting faces in granite

from the depression until the war, Nick and the men blasted
away, until they had revealed, who folks thought were the
greats
even T.R. made it in.

One wonders now, if Borglum was around and Nick was
above ground
Who they might say should be on Mt. Rushmore today or
would they just be

playing ball
unable to determine
or create consensus
that any of the last forty or so
were worthy of being dynamited
into posterity

Not Touched by a Woman

For a year
Not the regular kind, the one you do not pay
Who expects, dinners, and conversation
About everything
That matters to her
Shoes, her mother, her exes, other boyfriends, the latest play
And your money

All who will get laid eventually on some night when
The planets line up, in her chart and she
Did not fight with her brother, mother

Forget her Zoloft, primrose and that much required
Sleeping pill
None of it her fault but yours
And rightly so, honestly

All your buddies,lie about draining their
bottles of Viagra for 500 bucks a throw
which is one long, mostly unwanted erection
for four bucks a throw, since she doesn't care if he's a rock
or not, only that he cares, enough to gain entry to the
forbidden place, he so desires, to pay off his blood flow
and libido

Will that woman pursued through food and drink, conversation and
Wit, will warm those cold sheets, and leave a scent that will propel you to believe
you are not yet in hell

None of perfect form, no infinite perfection, nor perfectly breasted
only there for some moment, about to quickly pass
that you still can attract someone to bed, and you are not such a sorry ass

COWARDS OF US ALL

We are made of bone and blood, multilayered complexity
Not to be cowards
What is it then that constricts saying what is on a mind
With clarity
keeps us from wanting to shout down bullies, angry women,
wimps
Even the bosses who hold our crotches and whip us with
that
paycheck

The bravest are not always burly, thick wristed and strong
of anything but heart, always stepping forward, even in
doubt
or troubled
they have fears, often hidden behind eyes ostensibly focused
on the trivia of life, but, devoted instead to making their
will known,
no matter cost or consequence, so sure they are that courage
will prevail

masters of the universe in battle and business
never doubting their steps
only to be shaken, as are we all, by the vagaries of family,
the world lived close by that we cannot delegate, regulate

or control

reduced to being everyman over weddings, addictions, bad

choices

families can make cowards of us all

even of the bravest men

without sword or shield against the foe of blood relations

diminishing even the most brave and noble

faced by the commitment to care, house, and guide

others than ourselves

if they were not here, and we alone would be

would courage more emerge

or we still too afraid to rebel

against the forces that now compel

our silence

Out There by Orion's Belt

You can see only black space out by the middle star
Gaze at it as long as you can, break away, stop the car
Turn off Sinatra, ZZ Top, and let Don Henley just drift
away

Look up there where it is mostly dark, between the gleams,
Black and empty as you can conjure
Dark forces pulling dark matter, unknown why, yet
scientists try
Some unseen pulling your life apart at the seams
Hoping for some known force to adhere the pieces together
In a life spinning on an invisible axis
a constellation of loved and lost, colliding at warp speed
towards oblivion

out there is an order, light years away, from when
time began, all captured by Van Gogh, a glimpse of
points of light, swirling as it might, in this Milky Way
mocking not the order out in space, but the disorder
in us

the Starry Night is serene, a dream penetrating a windshield
stopped along Highway 101, and you a speck of protoplasm
wanting to be part of
it all

HE IS A DECENT MAN

Always paid the bills, put in the 14 hour day
Listened when he could to
Everyone
Daughters, sons, wives, mother and father while alive
All the aunts and uncles until they died
Attentive to the bosses needs
Bowing when required being sure to please

Righteous without virtue
Smoking rum soaked cigars
Lived the limousine life when it was there
Until it all dissolved into a struggle to survive
Then he became

Undernourished, hollow, emotionally starving
decent man,
seeking recognition, of his most basic wants
untouched, relic of another time and place
undulating towards a solitary chair facing a teevee
where the small world in it becomes his only unchallenged
domain

dreams now all abated, no longer contemplated
this decent man Oprahfied, harmonized to the them
in his life

deballed, debased, and denied
a deserved elevation of his kind contemplation,
of good heart, right thinking, hard working man

doing what he can to place everyone in the right place
see their needs and pleasures, while dodging the
big "C" stalking him, avoiding the coronary, hoping for
some more life to live decently.

THE HAND OF MARS

Is on the ass of Venus
Lavinia painted it that way
In 1595

He has dropped his sword and shield
Not needing them it seems to conquer a fully nude
And available Venus, who looks over her shoulder
At the soldiers right hand firmly on her left cheek

Yet he has failed to shed his helmet
Afraid perhaps to give up what authority he may possess
As warrior to goddess
His body is tan and ruddy, and only his loins are covered
Prepared he seems to conquer her

She possesses the smirk of women through the ages
Knowing, no matter how fierce this God of War
She will win the day, and decide when she is able to
offer him her play

Mars has his eyes transfixed on hers, even as her gaze seems
distracted and
almost looks away.
Only Lavinia knows who attacks whom.

OPEN COLLARED MEN

Sit on the stool at this stripper bar
named Cougar's
No chains on their necks anymore, no sweat on the chin
or brow
Relaxed, unrehearsed, with a perfect nonchalance
Puts 20's in her thong, gets a forehead kiss

For an hour or so, he greets old friends it seems
And the owners, dressed alike, offering bonhomie
A soda, and is pinned down by an assortment of leggy
Woman of all types, cups, and styles, most with
Pneumatic breasts and round, grand asses

All the men around, look the same, not a tie or buttoned
shirt
to be found, black T shirts for sure, and an assortment of
Khaki
and camo as well
construction, painters, clerks, cops, salesmen and even city
workers
this band of open collared men
mostly underappreciated, under screwed and underpaid

A full army of men who turn America on and off
every single day

take their wives to date movies, hate it though they do
love their kids and struggle to keep them going straight
tell their bosses what they must, to earn their trust

these open collared men always eulogized
when they all die too young as
"he was the salt of the earth"
Before they're buried in the ground

In a bar of strippers, with a fistful of presidents
Soliciting nothing more than a
Smile, a rub, a forehead kiss
And the fleeting freedom of the open collar life

CATSUP SANDWICH

When nothing aligns, it can seem that
You will always be hungry, sleepless most nights,
And alone
You can occupy your time in places where others dwell
classrooms, the library, a bus station and not feel like you
have entered
some specially designed hell

but that stomach growl is primal and gets all your attention
until you make it pass. And you can run out of cash, and
are too
proud or just afraid to beg
sit in a diner before there were fast food joints and steal
mustard jars
and bottles of Heinz
buy a loaf of white bread for 20 cents
and make a sandwich of it, lift a Coke from a trashcan out
back of the place
and call it dinner

and I had a job, used the money to buy books, and gas and
just make it through until the better job came along
which it did, when the busboy, caught me taking Heinz got
me a job

cooking and as a cashier,

hard lessons

even if you are faced with no one believing in you,

you cannot stop believing in yourself,

or you will expire,

and a mustard and catsup sandwich is not the worst of things.

ZEN CODE

Zen has no code as such

It is to be, where nothing adheres

But clarity

Not like Ecclesiastes where all is vanity and

A striving after the wind

Zen is the realization that all is Mushin, or Wuxin

Nothingness

And a special way to be

Where you can move freely towards any objective

With no notions preconceived

Zoned in, in modern speech and thought

Fluid in movement, and response, able to act unattached to

Old techniques, philosophies, or winds of change

And all the sages rag

Before enlightenment, chop wood, carry water

After enlightenment, chop wood, carry water

The day to day does not expire as you aspire

Whatever perceived height you achieve

You always wear the white belt again

The real masters are novices repeatedly

On your way to a Zen code you may find

You are most aligned when you have control of your life

Are part of a family or tradition
And never end becoming a master of the task you have set
before you
to mark progress

Everything is Zen or not Zen
The pursuit of nothingness is an extraordinary something
That can become your greatest gift to yourself
And the world you populate

I Swept the Floors

That summer of '62 by the driving range
of a public course walked over a few miles
from home, took the bus back, covered in
garbage and smelling of crap

had a specific route assigned by the club pro
who ran the concession stand as well
cleaned out the 14 garbage cans every hour
took the broom to the café and the hallway
in front of the bathroom stalls

on Saturday, I brought a clean collared shirt to wear
so I could soda jerk the counter, serving up soda after
I filled the tanks with syrup and attached the CO_2
Chatted up the golfers wives, in their short tennis skirts
setting my intentions on their daughters too
some clown would always pull a joke just to show me
who was
the higher class, and I piled high extra scoops to impress
their
lazy asses, and for a buck tip

I swept the floor and listened to all they had to say
of big deals coming by next Saturday,
heard them whine over who was

Mayor and who they would lay next Wednesday,
and sometimes
read their magazines discarded after they evacuated,
breakfast and lunch
into a toilet bowl

Honest work, for enough pay, all cash, under the table
what I learned at the end of that
broom that summer only made me wiser
ripened my view of the way of men with colored pants and
green in their pockets
and took a silent oath to never push a broom again

No Heroes Here

Never had a hero to compel me
No Superman or Hercules
Mantle, Marris, or even Wilt
Audie Murphy or Marciano
Admired though they were, I found no perfect model
to become or emulate, although I yearned to find just one
who could show me some perfect path of what I could
become

Certainly men I did revere in business and sport
Thinkers, philosophers, and many other sorts
Challenged to create, survive, or display courage
under fire, all I studied, reviewed and analyzed
to autopsy what they had inside that made them
uncommon, so I could emulate, duplicate, evaluate
just what they had inside

Ruth, Cy Young, Cobb, and Robinson
Chamberlin, Dr. J, the Big O, West, Pat Riley,
Lombardi, of course, and Landry, Namath and Y.A.,
Bradshaw, Young, and
Montana, not likely to name them all
Ash, Poncho, Laver, and McEnroe
Thorpe, Spitz, Jenner, Phelps totally smooth and sublime

Johnson, Louis, Ali, Rocky, the real one, Patterson, and Sugar Ray

Patton, Ike, Bradley, Marshall, and Vinegar Joe, of WWII and Washington
before, warriors and good men, not one totally rotten

Hemingway, Steinbeck, Michener, Roth and Mailer

Duke, Lancaster, Kirk, Peck, Holden, Stewart, Cooper, Pacino, Steiger
and Marlon, Clint, I can't forget

Bukowski, Fante, Blake, Murakami, Christopherson, Cash, Proust, The Bard,

Frankl, Freud, Jung, and even old Ayn Rand

Every Mayor I ever met from Coleman Young to Frank Rizzo

A priest or two, Reagan, Ford, and Clinton who all had outstretched hands
a word or two to share
Only one likeable millionaire
and a CIA assassin who is just a regular guy without his gun

And my father

Jungle fighter, at war, working man, at Sears for 37 years,
The true heart of gold, loved by everyman, buried him and
his dreams
unrevealed,
gave away his life to everyone else, retaining nothing for
himself
selfless

All had something to offer or a piece to glean
rarely to internalize, because they were just not me
extraordinary in their way, otherwise just as flawed or
more by
the foibles shared within, all with grand destiny, perhaps,
but not one
free of flesh, hubris, or sin.

What is then a man without heroes
Just another man, hoping to be an inspiration
To someone

AT VICTOR'S BEFORE
THE OSCARS

Across from the Scientology Center
Where people get clear
Victor's booths are full by noon, no one rushing to
Pick up a tuxedo or some outrageous dress to sashay
Along a carpet dyed red, rolled out for one over amped night
Celebrating how one performance can rise to be seen
above the
complexity and collaboration that creates the cinema dreams

Actors, when they are not waiters come
Unshaven here
In workingmen caps and flannel shirts
Sit with adenoidal mouths, coughing, sniffing,
rubbing, just opened eyes at noon the winter day
before the big dance
Always laughing loudly, speaking in conspiratorial tones to
cellphones
With an agent, screaming from her estate at them
Talent here without a stage, slurping through matzo balled
chicken
soup, snorting back a lunger, acting out "disgusting" for
some future
Golden Globe

surrounded by the aroma of passable Joe fueling great expectations

Boys, they are really with straight teeth, full lips and manicured fingers

Women with eyeglasses pushed into their bleached hair, long nails

done French style with white caps

moving their bony arms through the air, perfumed with maple syrup

conducting their life stories, replete with trivial matters writ large and plenty

of embellished "petty miseries"

One afternoon before the poseurs sway before a nation

celebrating, what they paid to see, from behind a tub of stale popcorn

Now, here conversing with a once Oscar winning writer, now has been, and reminiscing

about a buddy who ate blintzes here covered in strawberry jam, who wrote,

spoke, created more and better stuff, was well liked, well paid, usually,

and memorialized when he rolled over dead alone, by the New York types

that these actors here, would kill to see

On their way these actors, in this cramped café, convinced mightily

They have something to offer and say

Besides their obvious bravado,schemes, manicured nails, and straight teeth

How far away can that carpet be

anyway

Are we clear?

How I learned to Stop Wasting Time and Appreciate Existence

By reading 3,000 pages A la recherché du temps perdu

For decades, I avoided writing for anything but work

Thought it an indulgence, that I would turn indolent or worse

Afraid of facing Hemingway's, "White Bull", the frightening empty

page

Ministered to a career, families came together only to be upended,

dutifully engaged in serious work, with humor only unintended

dabbled when the forces hit, storm clouds releasing all their rage,

avoided a certain "knowing" that it was something I must do

and it bothered me through all of life's tumults, and tears

A small hand of fate dropped Proust on me, In Search of Lost Time,

this frail son of the doctor who destroyed cholera in France
who did nothing more,this jobless flaneur, than put his memory to work
on one timeless tome, all 3,000 pages of it, that I started reading one winter's
night, until Easter came .

Compelled he was to surmise some meaning in his life, without the distractions of
Internet, movies, television and such, he designed a narrative for his time
Lost to me his view of meaning that emanates from
social status, love in all its twists,
And art or habits filling up one's time

Involuntary memory was not a waste of time, it seemed, opening
his insides

William Blake suggests if you "refuse and bury" talent, "shame and confusion
of face will pursue him throughout life to eternity"

That's if you have talent, in some measure, or more likely for me
endurance, focus, and the willpower to sit for hours and compose

a thought that might resonate, strike some chord, console, challenge,
divide or bridge the gap between what is and might be

Of all the writer's tools Hemingway lamented
Is a "shit detector" built in and shock proof
I've that
And memories mine and imagined, required
Says Murakami
"an endless battle of contrasting memories"

It is now my greatest vice, and on occasion great pleasure
more often wonderment watching words take shape out
of some obscure and private place
It is a race without a finish line, and only death can stop it.
ENOUGH for now.

Printed in the United States
By Bookmasters